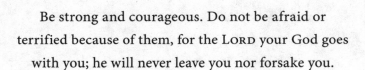

Be strong and courageous. Do not be afraid or terrified because of them, for the LORD your God goes with you; he will never leave you nor forsake you.

—DEUTERONOMY 31:6 (NIV)

MYSTERIES OF COBBLE HILL FARM

MYSTERIES OF COBBLE HILL FARM

Into Thin Air

SANDRA ORCHARD

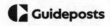

Mysteries of Cobble Hill Farm is a trademark of Guideposts.

Published by Guideposts
100 Reserve Road, Suite E200
Danbury, CT 06810
Guideposts.org

This is a work of fiction. While the setting of Mysteries of Cobble Hill Farm as presented in this series is fictional, the location of Yorkshire, England, actually exists, and some places and characters may be based on actual places and people whose identities have been used with permission or fictionalized to protect their privacy. Apart from the actual people, events, and locales that figure into the fiction narrative, all other names, characters, businesses, and events are the creation of the author's imagination and any resemblance to actual persons or events is coincidental.

Every attempt has been made to credit the sources of copyrighted material used in this book. If any such acknowledgment has been inadvertently omitted or miscredited, receipt of such information would be appreciated.

Scripture references are from the following sources: *The Holy Bible, King James Version* (KJV). *The Holy Bible, New International Version* (NIV). Copyright © 1973, 1978, 1984, 2011 by Biblica, Inc. Used by permission of Zondervan. All rights reserved worldwide. www.zondervan.com.

Cover and interior design by Müllerhaus
Cover illustration by Bob Kayganich at Illustration Online LLC.
Typeset by Aptara, Inc.

ISBN 978-1-961126-92-3 (hardcover)
ISBN 978-1-961251-44-1 (softcover)
ISBN 978-1-961126-93-0 (epub)

Printed and bound in the United States of America
10 9 8 7 6 5 4 3 2 1

MYSTERIES OF COBBLE HILL FARM

Into Thin Air

GLOSSARY OF UK TERMS

beck • a creek

brass • British slang for money, typically coins

brown sauce • a condiment usually made of a combination of tomatoes, malt vinegar, molasses, dates, spices, and tamarind.

fair geffered • exhausted

gimmer • a year-old ewe

loo • restroom

mithering • annoying

nob • a person from the upper class

pinder • a person whose job it is to deal with stray animals

rambler • walker or hiker

wellies • Wellington boots

CHAPTER ONE

Harriet Bailey smiled at the sight of the young boy sitting in the waiting room of Cobble Hill Veterinary Clinic on Friday morning, a docile hen roosting contentedly on his lap. "Come on in, Allen. How is Rosie doing?"

The boy sprang to his feet. "Right as rain, Miss Harriet. She's mighty grateful for us saving her. She's laid a double-yolk egg every day since. I candled them to see." He was referring to the practice of holding an egg up to a candle or other light source to see what was inside without cracking it.

Laughing, Harriet lifted the hen out of the boy's arms, being careful of its splinted leg. "Wow, that's high praise."

The boy grabbed an egg carton from the seat beside the one he'd vacated then followed Harriet to an exam room. "I brought you a bunch. Not all Rosie's, since I wanted to give you a full dozen, but some of hers are in here."

"Thank you so much. I appreciate that."

Rosie pecked at Harriet's dangling ponytail.

Harriet deposited the inquisitive hen on the examination table then flicked her ponytail behind her shoulder and tucked the stray tendrils of dark brown hair behind her ears. "She certainly seems spry enough."

"She is. The other hens tried to peck at her splint, so I've kept her penned away from them, close to the house. And I visit her every day."

"I'm sure she loves all the attention." Chickens didn't always appreciate the ministrations of rambunctious young boys, but Harriet had witnessed Allen's extraordinary care and been impressed. She removed the splint from the bird's leg and examined it carefully.

Allen had raced over on his sister's bicycle a few weeks ago with the hen in the basket on the bike's handlebars. "I need to see the new lady vet," he'd blurted to Polly Thatcher at the reception desk. He said a fox had gotten into the hen's enclosure and injured Rosie before he could chase it away. To make matters worse, Rosie was his mother's favorite hen.

Harriet's heart warmed at the memory of the confidence the boy had placed in her capabilities. Several of the local farmers, especially the old-timers, were still wary of the idea of a *lady* vet—and an American at that—taking over her beloved grandfather's decades-old veterinary practice in the heart of North Yorkshire.

Harriet stroked Rosie's feathers. "I'm pleased with how her leg has mended. She shouldn't have any trouble with it now."

"I'm most grateful to you, Doc."

"It's been my pleasure."

He stuffed his hands deep into his jean pockets. "What do I owe you?"

Harriet glanced at the carton of eggs he'd set on her counter and knew exactly how her grandfather would respond. "Those farm-fresh eggs should cover it."

"Really?" He picked up Rosie and hugged her to his chest. "Oh, thank you! My dad said she weren't worth the coin it'd cost to mend her. But after she started laying double-yolkers, even he admitted she's a right grand hen."

Harriet chuckled. "I'm glad to hear it. She is indeed grand." She opened the door for him and gave a relieved sigh at the empty waiting room. After spending half the night seeing to a sick calf, she desperately needed coffee. As fond as she'd grown of the locals' strong Yorkshire tea, she needed a bigger caffeine kick before facing the rest of her day.

As if she'd read her mind, Polly exchanged a mug of coffee for the carton of eggs Harriet held. The spunky twenty-four-year-old had been her grandfather's receptionist and assistant, and she'd happily stayed on to help when Harriet inherited his practice. She had also become a good friend.

"Do you have a date?" Harriet gestured to Polly's long dark hair, which had been hanging loose when Allen arrived with Rosie and was now styled in a casual updo. Harriet suspected a fair number of the young men who happened into the clinic with stray cats came in the hope of asking Polly out.

Polly fanned the loose tendrils still hanging about her neck. "No, just overheated. I pulled a couple of fans out of the supply cupboard, but they don't help much. I know it's August, but I can't remember it ever being this hot."

"Yeah, with Yorkshire being on the North Sea, I didn't expect to miss air-conditioning. It was never this hot when I visited Grandad in the summer as a kid. Even the beach was chilly."

Polly grimaced. "Until the last year or two, we never thought we'd need air-conditioning here. We considered hot weather a treat. And I know drinking hot coffee doesn't help, but you looked as if you needed it."

"I did. Thanks."

When Harriet's grandfather, Harold Bailey, passed away late last year, he'd left Cobble Hill Farm to Harriet, including the veterinary practice housed in the north end of the farm's two-hundred-year-old, two-story stone house where multiple generations of Baileys had been raised. The large property, surrounded by rolling dales dotted with sheep and cattle hemmed in by Yorkshire's iconic drystone walls, was about a mile north of the village of White Church Bay.

Still carrying the egg carton, Polly pushed through the door at the end of a short hallway behind the reception desk, which opened into the home kitchen. "I'm glad to see you at least got a dozen eggs out of Allen for your services this time." Her eyes twinkled with amusement when she glanced back over her shoulder.

Harriet trailed after her. "I couldn't very well have charged him for putting a splint on a chicken leg. Imagine what the farmers would have said about me. Besides, you know Grandad would have done the same thing." She'd gone through some of his records. Old Doc Bailey had frequently accepted barter in lieu of money for his services.

"Aye." Polly feigned a thick Yorkshire accent. "The lass put a splint on the bird's leg then made the lad pay more brass than he'd pay for a dressed chicken."

Harriet scarcely managed to swallow her swig of coffee without spurting it out on a laugh. "Exactly."

"Just wait," Polly warned, turning serious. "Once your soft spot for distressed youngsters gets out, our waiting room will be full of them with all manner of pets. And eggs won't pay the electricity bill, let alone the updates this place needs."

Snagging a cookie from the biscuit tin, Harriet groaned, all too aware that more than a few of her grandfather's once-regular farm clients had yet to avail themselves of her services. "I thought I struck a good deal with young Alfie when he offered to feed and water any animals in our care in exchange for the medication for his sister's cat."

"He's a good kid." It had certainly been a nice break for Harriet and Polly with more clients boarding their dogs during summer holidays, not to mention the donkey.

At the sound of Harriet fiddling with the biscuit tin, Maxwell clattered into the kitchen to mooch one, with Charlie not far behind. The dog and cat had come with the clinic. Maxwell was an adorable long-haired dachshund whose hind legs were paralyzed when he was hit by a car. Nevertheless, he happily motored around the place with a wheeled prosthesis that Harriet's grandfather had gotten for him.

Charlie had been rescued from a burning trash bin as a kitten. Her coat was patchy due to scars from the fire, but what there was of it bore soft-hued patches of gray, ginger, and white, which Harriet would call a muted calico. Harriet's grandfather had named all the clinic's adopted felines "Charlie" regardless of the cat's gender, claiming it was one less thing he had to remember.

Harriet treated Maxwell to a dog biscuit and Charlie to a fish-flavored cat treat. Maxwell practically inhaled his snack, but Charlie took her time examining the offering before she deigned to accept it from Harriet's fingers.

Polly helped herself to a cookie too. "At least the income from your grandfather's art gallery is helping make up for any shortfall."

Besides being a beloved country vet, Harriet's grandfather had become an accomplished painter of both animals and gorgeous scenes of the area's landscapes. He had opened the Bailey Art Gallery in the former carriage house on the property to showcase his work—a gallery that he had also bequeathed to Harriet, who had opened it up to visitors again last month.

"The write-up that blogger did on the discovery of the Henderson painting has boosted interest in the farm. Mrs. Winslow told me the number of visitors to the gallery has doubled and prints of Grandad's most popular paintings and other artsy souvenirs are flying off the shelves." Mrs. Ida Winslow had run the gallery since its opening and had graciously agreed to continue to manage it for Harriet.

"Yeah, and it isn't even going on display until next weekend." The blogger who'd offered to feature the gallery was Callum Henderson-Grainger, the grandson of the deceased farmer who'd left the painting to the gallery in his will. At first, Harriet had been worried Callum's request for a tour and interview was a ploy to convince her that the painting should remain in *his* family. The painting had, after all, been a gift from her grandfather to Callum's great-grandfather, long before Harold Bailey's paintings garnered national acclaim. But Callum hadn't so much as hinted that he wanted the painting for himself.

The gallery earned a reasonable amount from sales of souvenirs and Grandad's prints, and a donations box at the gallery entrance helped offset overhead costs, such as utilities and pest control and paying Mrs. Winslow to monitor the comings and goings of visitors.

Harriet swallowed the last of her coffee. "Do I have time to check in with the pest control guys before our next appointment?"

"You're done here for today. Unless an emergency call comes in, your afternoon is wide open."

"That's not a good sign." Not that a healthy pet population was a bad thing, if that was *all* that was keeping clients at home. "This makes two days in a row with no farm calls, not counting last night's emergency. Although at least yesterday's quiet schedule can be blamed on the Yorkshire Day celebrations."

"That's true enough."

Yorkshire folks were fiercely proud of their county's heritage and had been officially celebrating that fact on the first day of August for almost fifty years. Polly had even dragged Harriet to the town's local pub to hear the reading of "a declaration of the integrity of Yorkshire." She'd been fascinated to learn that the county's rich history could be traced back to the first millennium. In fact, the stone wall around the city of York had been standing for more than 1,100 years.

"I better go see how Rhys and Ronnie are doing." Harriet started out the clinic door that opened to the practice's parking area and almost bowled over a young woman carrying a ginger-haired, chubby-cheeked infant in a car seat. "I'm so sorry. I didn't see you there."

"No, it's my fault." The woman smoothed her hair. "I should have knocked."

Harriet held the door open and motioned her inside. When no pets followed, she asked the woman, "How may I help you?"

"We're here to see Dr. Garrett for my baby's eight-week checkup."

"I see." Harriet's aunt, Jinny Garrett, was the town's local physician. "Her office is in the dower cottage off the far end of the parking area."

Both homes sat well back from the road, so a client coming up the long driveway would first pass the carriage-house-turned-art-gallery on the right with the handful of parking spaces opposite it before reaching the larger parking area that served both Aunt Jinny's and the veterinary practices. Harriet's place stood on the right, and the dower house sat at a right angle to it at the end of the parking lot, with the entrance facing the road and the rear of the cottage offering a spectacular view of the North Sea.

A large meadow provided a buffer between the houses and the cliffside, and colorful, flower-filled gardens, like little sanctuaries, furnished green space between the buildings. Harriet especially appreciated the low stone wall around the property. A narrow lane perpendicular to the driveway ran past the gallery and around to the barn.

"I went to Dr. Garrett's first," the woman explained, "but the sign on her door said she was called to an emergency and won't be back for half an hour. I was hoping I might use your loo while I wait."

"Of course. It's right through there."

"You can leave the baby with us," Polly volunteered, clearing off a table to make room for the infant's car seat. "I wouldn't want you to put him on the floor with all the dogs and cats we get traipsing through here."

"I hadn't thought of that. Thank you." The woman set the car seat in the middle of the table. "Mummy will be right back," she whispered to the sleeping baby.

The moment she disappeared through the door, Polly let out a squeal. "Isn't he adorable?"

The baby's eyes popped open, and when they locked onto Polly, his bottom lip began to quiver.

"Oh, no. Don't cry, sweetheart." Polly unbuckled him. "Your mummy will be back before you know it."

"What are you doing?" Harriet asked.

"Taking him out before he starts crying." She lifted him to her shoulder, carefully supporting his head. "There, there. It's all right," Polly reassured him in a singsong that could charm the most nervous feline.

Unfortunately, the baby didn't share their clients' temperaments. His whimpers turned to wails.

Polly bounced gently, shushing him.

It didn't work.

"You know what they say," Harriet quipped. "Let sleeping dogs lie. I guess the same applies to babies."

"I can't understand it. The kids at the church's Bible camp love me."

"That's because you bring puppies and lambs to help tell your stories."

"You might be right." Polly lifted the infant off her shoulder and held him out to Harriet. "Here, you have a go."

Harriet cuddled the child and began humming a lullaby she remembered her mom singing to her when she was little.

He quieted immediately.

"Ah, you have the touch," Polly proclaimed.

Smiling, Harriet inhaled, savoring the sweet baby scent. If her fiancé hadn't broken off their engagement, they might have soon been welcoming a little bundle of joy like this into their lives. She swallowed the bitter taste that rose in her throat at how Dustin Stewart's rejection had not only ended their upcoming wedding and her dreams of starting a family but robbed her of a job too, since there'd been no way she could have continued to work in the same veterinary practice as him.

She gently swayed in rhythm as she continued to hum, reminding herself that she'd forgiven Dustin. After all, if he hadn't ended things, she might never have left Connecticut and traveled halfway around the world to Cobble Hill Farm to take over her grandfather's veterinary practice.

"I'm sorry, did he get fussy?" The woman's voice jolted Harriet from her thoughts.

"It's no problem. He's a lovely boy." Harriet carefully handed the content child to his mother. "You're welcome to wait here for Dr. Garrett if you like. We don't have air-conditioning, but it's a little cooler in here than outside."

"It's kind of you to offer, but there's a lovely breeze coming in off the bay. Now that Benji's awake, I can show him the neighbor's lambs."

"Mind you don't get too close to their alpacas. They like to spit," Polly cautioned.

The woman chuckled. "I'll remember that. Thank you."

Harriet turned to Polly. "I'm going to speak to the pest control guys. Feel free to close the office early today if you'd like. Just be sure to forward office calls to my cell phone."

"You got it."

Harriet waved to the young mother and hurried toward the art gallery.

Ronnie and Rhys of Reynolds Pest Removal Company were on ladders, removing ivy from the side of the building. The bare stone wall wasn't nearly as aesthetic as it had appeared when covered in lush greenery, but Ronnie had explained that they needed to remove everything that made it easy for the squirrels to climb to the roof and burrow in the attic. The destructive rodents had already caused enough damage. She was grateful she'd found a company that would remove them humanely. Gray squirrels were persona non grata, or rather *anima non grata* in Britain, since they'd driven the native red squirrel to the brink of extinction after being brought to the country in the 1800s.

"How goes the battle?" she called up to Ronnie.

The lanky man, who appeared closer in age to Polly's twenty-four years than Harriet's thirty-three, removed his tweed flat cap and clutched it to his chest as he met Harriet's gaze. "Those squirrels are right stubborn, and I'm fair geffered from the mithering task."

Harriet blinked, her mind whirling. *Geffered? Mithering?*

"But don't worry," he went on. "She'll be right by the time we're done. We'll catch all the rascals."

Don't worry, she mentally repeated, nodding. Despite having lived in the UK for months now, she still struggled to decipher what many of the locals said.

"Excuse me." A gray-haired man waved to Harriet from the pasture on the other side of the driveway. "Is this the Bailey Art Gallery?"

"It is indeed."

The man and his female companion made their way through the turnstile, referred to by the locals as a kissing gate, that ensured farm animals didn't escape the pasture. Each day, at least a few visitors arrived at the farm via the public pathway that traversed the moors and linked up with the coast-to-coast trail along the cliffside. The pair hurried across the drive, walking sticks in each hand and sizable rucksacks—backpacks—on their backs.

Harriet pointed out the way then grabbed her ringing phone. The office number appeared on the screen. "Polly, I thought I told you to take the rest of the day off."

"I was about to when an emergency call came in. Ned Staveley at Goose Beck Farm on Harbottom Road has a sick cow and needs you to come out. I'll text directions."

"Appreciate it. You can let him know I'm on my way." Harriet hurried to her vehicle, an ancient green Land Rover she'd not so affectionately dubbed "the Beast." She'd inherited it along with the practice. While climbing in, she saw the woman who had brought her baby into the clinic furtively duck into the trees.

But where was her baby?

CHAPTER TWO

Hope sparked in Harriet's chest as she drove. Mr. Staveley was a prosperous cattle farmer who had previously eschewed her services in favor of a vet from Whitby, despite having been her grandfather's client for decades. If she could save his cow and earn his respect, she might finally turn the tide of opinion among the older farmers.

She ground the stick shift into a lower gear for the steep incline. She'd developed nerves of steel driving these roads in the past few months. She'd even gotten over her nervousness with round-abouts, actually preferring them to stop signs or traffic lights, since they kept traffic moving and made driving a manual transmission a whole lot easier than it would be if she had to stop at every intersection.

She wished street name signs, when they existed, were mounted higher up instead of at waist level. Finding her clients was difficult enough with names like Goose Beck Farm rather than street numbers.

Not that having a street number would help much. Her phone's map app inevitably went haywire at some point along the route. It either lost the signal due to the terrain or directed her to a different farm than where she was meant to be. And it was a hundred times worse when she was called out at night with no streetlights illuminating the intersections. It was funny, the things she'd taken for granted back home.

Back in Connecticut, she corrected. Cobble Hill Farm, which sat above the Yorkshire village of White Church Bay, was home now.

She wound her way down a steep, twisting lane and over a bridge, and then she shifted again and held her breath the entire climb up the even steeper hill on the other side. The first time she'd faced a hill like this, which they'd kindly marked with gradient signs, she'd been woefully naive. Twenty-two percent didn't sound like a particularly steep incline—until you were halfway up in a vehicle that had long since lost the momentum it started up with. These days she had a bit more confidence that the Beast could handle the incline, but she didn't want to overtax the old girl.

She passed over a cattle grid and mentally ran through the illnesses that cows were prone to this time of year. "August bag," the farmers' colloquial term for mastitis, was a common and potentially devastating situation. It was spread by flies and could affect any cow, even bulls, although dry cows and in-calf heifers were predominantly hit. Harriet wished Polly had gotten more details on the phone. While speedy administration of anti-inflammatories and antibiotics could typically save the cow, a quarter of the bag affected was usually lost. Not an ideal outcome for her first visit.

Harriet shook her head. A farmer like Ned Staveley, living near water with the summer weather they'd had, would have taken the necessary precautions of treating his herd long before the flies had a chance to cause problems.

She scanned the fields on either side for signs of the house and barns. With so much common grazing land in the area, spotting the farm should be an easy task. But the drystone walls and hedges hemming the fields made the driveways easy to miss until she was almost upon them.

The undulating hills weren't as lush as they'd been when she arrived in the spring, but the bilberry bushes were producing their tangy fruit. Darkening blue berries dotted the low-lying shrubs, similar to the blueberries she was used to but stronger in flavor. In another couple of weeks, the heather would bloom and paint the fields a glorious purple. Inhaling deeply, she revisited their light floral scent with musky undertones from her childhood summer romps through the moors.

The whistles, chirrups, and twitters of various birds drifted through her open windows, occasionally punctuated by a cock pheasant's distinctive call. She really couldn't ask for a more pleasant break than driving through the countryside, even on a muggy, overcast day like this one. Granted, come winter she might not feel quite so enthusiastic about navigating the back country roads, but she was used to driving in harsh winter weather. It was the foggy weather she dreaded most.

The road narrowed to scarcely more than the Land Rover's width, and she tightened her grip on the steering wheel as a car approached from the opposite direction. She'd become adept at spotting safe spots to pull over to allow an oncoming vehicle to pass, although occasionally her timing was a little off and she found herself holding her breath as her side mirrors all but scraped the stone wall or the passing car or both.

This time, the car passed by without incident, the driver offering her a friendly wave as he passed.

Soon grazing sheep gave way to grazing cattle, and Harriet figured she was close to the Staveley farm. If the sick cow had recently calved, she could be facing a mineral deficiency or perhaps a pinched nerve or injured pelvis.

Spotting a farm gate in the stone wall ahead, Harriet slowed the vehicle. An old barn stood a couple of hundred yards from the road at the end of a rutted cart path, but it stood alone—no houses or farmer in sight.

Arriving at a farm to discover the patient and the farmer were nowhere to be found was the bane of country vets. But farms usually identified themselves with a sign at least, and this lone barn had none, so she drove on.

Less than a mile down the road, a pond came into view. Numerous Canadian geese and several pairs of white geese floated about on the water or ambled along the shore. But the peaceful setting wasn't enough to calm her racing thoughts when she spotted the sign identifying the place as Goose Beck Farm.

Harriet proceeded up the long drive, gamely negotiating the ruts while scanning the outbuildings for signs of her client.

An older Yorkshire farmer, barrel-chested with suspenders—or what the locals called braces—holding up his trousers, strode out of the stone barn and waited for her to park. "You must be the new Doc Bailey," he bellowed. "I recognize Harold's truck."

Harriet grabbed her bag and jumped from the vehicle. "Yes, I'm Harriet Bailey." She extended her hand. "Are you Mr. Staveley?"

"That's me." He wiped his large hand on a rag hanging from his belt loop then gave her a hearty handshake. "This way, lass."

She tried not to cringe at the address. More than one farmer had questioned her capabilities as a farm vet, given the degree of strength often required to work with large animals and the fact she was a somewhat petite woman. But Mr. Staveley didn't sound as if he meant anything negative by addressing her the way he did.

Since moving here she'd been called duck, love, and lass in equal measure. Although duck was the oddest of the names, she was kind of partial to it, remembering that her grandfather had called her duckie on her childhood visits.

"What are we dealing with? And when did the symptoms start?"

"A calf." He led Harriet into the barn and motioned toward the first stall. "I spotted him in the pasture this morning. He seemed poorly, staggering about as if he couldn't keep his feet."

Harriet was grateful Mr. Staveley had taken the step of bringing the calf inside, sparing her from coping with an irate mama and inquisitive herd mates. She could hear the little fellow's mother lowing from somewhere nearby. The calf's coat was a light gold color, and an adorable mop of hair already sprouted from the top of his head between his horns, nearly covering his eyes. As they joined him in the stall, he bumped into the wall, which was unusual for a calf his age.

The Staveleys raised Highland cattle, a hardy, stocky breed with sharp horns and thick, hairy coats. The breed was a great choice for grazing on the moors—not aggressive unless their calves were threatened, and otherwise curious and friendly.

Observing the calf, Harriet's first suspicion was that he had perennial ryegrass staggers, with its symptoms of stumbling, stiffness, irregular eye movements, and head shaking. Ryegrass was plentiful in the moorland. It was usually good forage for livestock, unless infected with a specific fungus that caused the staggers.

Harriet took the calf's vitals and checked him over. In addition to the obvious loss of coordination, his eyelids twitched spastically, he had muscle tremors, and he frothed at the mouth. "How is his appetite?"

"He isn't bawling for his mum, and he's not eating the hay I gave him."

Harriet examined his hooves and then ran her hands down his legs once more. "There's no sign that he's impaled himself on a rusty nail or old wire, which is good." The symptoms could fit a number of conditions at this point, including mineral deficiency. But that tended to afflict the mothers, thanks to the high demands placed on them to feed their young. "How is the calf's mother?"

"Right as rain."

"Is it possible he got into something he shouldn't have out in the field?" While farmers were conscientious about not leaving something as sweetly attractive and deadly as antifreeze lying about, they didn't always think about the potential damage that old farm equipment and the like could inflict.

"They've been grazing the common land."

In other words, it was unlikely. "And this is the only animal that's sick?"

"So far."

She moved to the barn window and squinted at the hills dotted with cattle. "Have you noticed any plants poisonous to cows growing in the fields?" Generally, grazing animals avoided poisonous plants, but a young calf might not eat as discriminately.

"Not any that the cows pay mind to," Mr. Staveley said.

Three curious young faces popped up between the stall's wooden slats. She'd grown used to the occasional audience, but these children seemed too young to be Mr. Staveley's. Grandchildren, perhaps.

Harriet mused over what the farmer had told her. The calf's symptoms pointed to lead poisoning. "He could simply be manifesting a vitamin deficiency, but the neurological signs suggest he might have ingested something poisonous. I can't be sure without a blood test." And with it being Friday, they wouldn't get the results for days.

"In the meantime, he gets sicker. And by the time the test comes back, it's too late to be of any good," the farmer fretted. "I'm certain there's nothing growing in the field that shouldn't be." He turned to the children. "Is there?"

"No, nothing," the oldest boy replied.

"They've been running the fields all summer. They'd have seen if something was growing there that shouldn't be."

The children nodded so earnestly that Harriet was inclined to doubt her gut. The lack of a fever and gastrointestinal upset ruled out a couple of possibilities. She needed to do more research. She inspected the calf's tongue and mouth then scoured his entire hide for evidence of a cut or sore that might have become infected. Finding nothing, she wondered if her grandfather's journals would give her insight into the situation.

"Well?" the farmer prodded.

She needed to treat the poor thing. "Until we know what's causing the symptoms, you should keep him quarantined. And I'd recommend checking the fields to see what he might've gotten into. I'll give him an injection for possible deficiencies and another with anti-inflammatories that should help with the stiffness. It would help if I could take a blood test." She looked at him expectantly.

The man frowned. "Are you sure that would tell you anything?"

Harriet sighed. "We can wait a bit, but if he doesn't show any improvement by morning, we should do the test."

The man's expression communicated loud and clear that he wasn't happy with her lack of definite answers or the prospect of more costly visits and tests with little to show for them.

"Have you given him any vaccines or antibiotics recently?" Most commercial farmers administered both themselves, ideally in consultation with a vet. But they often accumulated a stockpile that they kept for emergencies or minor situations that they could deal with themselves.

The man hooked his thumbs in his braces. "I've given him nothing."

Harriet murmured acknowledgment as she administered the injections. "If he shows no sign of improvement by morning, I'll come by to collect a blood sample and start a course of antibiotics."

The man grunted, which she took as agreement.

She didn't need to reiterate the importance of keeping the calf quarantined. In his years as a farmer, Mr. Staveley would have seen enough epidemics sweep through herds to know the precautions inside and out. In fact, it had likely been a fear of BSE, more commonly known as mad cow disease, that had spurred him to call her. Not that they had a reliable test for the disease in a live cow.

Thankfully, she was confident they weren't facing a resurgence of that dreaded disease. Nor another foot-and-mouth outbreak like those that had gutted too many Yorkshire farms. "Please phone the clinic in the morning to let me know how he's doing either way."

Once again, she took his grunt as agreement. As she packed up her bag, she second-guessed not insisting on taking a blood test right away. Although, given the time, the lab wouldn't be open to receive it until morning anyway. With any luck, the injections she'd administered would do the trick, and she'd be the first vet he called from here on out.

She smiled at the children as she passed them and climbed into her vehicle. But when she turned the key in the ignition, the truck wouldn't start. She glanced at the farmer and kids, who had all lined up outside the barn to watch her departure. Realizing she hadn't fully depressed the clutch on the first go, she tried again. This time the engine started, but the truck immediately lurched forward.

She slammed the brake, lambasting herself for forgetting to put the gearshift in neutral. The third time was the charm, and she managed to get herself turned around and down the driveway.

But the instant she pulled onto the road, her facade of confidence drooped along with her shoulders. She cringed at the grinding noise that accompanied a clumsy shift. She looked in her rearview mirror and winced at the sight of them all still watching her. Mr. Staveley was probably thinking that if her driving skills were any indication of her veterinary skills, his calf was in serious trouble.

CHAPTER THREE

When Harriet neared Cobble Hill Farm, she encountered a line of cars parked on the too-narrow lane and had to gingerly maneuver past them. What on earth were all these people doing here? A public footpath crossed the farm's second field, but she'd never seen hikers' cars lining the lane. She turned into the drive and encountered two dozen more cars squeezed into the farm's parking area.

No way could Aunt Jinny's patient backlog account for so many vehicles, and she doubted they were all tourists here to see her grandfather's art gallery. In his later years, his paintings had earned him national and even international acclaim after a royal interview had been filmed with one of his paintings on a castle wall in the background. It was a pastoral painting of border collies herding sheep in the dales, and the exposure skyrocketed interest in his art, and, by extension, his entire life's work, including the farm and veterinary practice. Harriet imagined the response then had been similar to what was happening now, but she couldn't begin to guess the reason this time.

She veered off the drive onto the grass to park near the barn and made a mental note to paint a large sign designating a portion of the parking lot for veterinary use only.

Several children raced out of the barn. Harriet leaped from the truck. "Hey, hold up. What were you kids doing in there?"

"Looking for animals," an eager little boy declared.

"Where are your parents?"

"In the barn," another child called over her shoulder as the group raced away.

Generally speaking, Harriet loved to see children excited to see the animals, but not when parents were seemingly oblivious to the whereabouts of their adventurous offspring.

They got city folk who thought nothing of allowing their dogs to run around off leash, especially when rambling on the public footpath through the fields. While most managed to keep their dogs close by, others thought it was cute to watch their dogs "play" with the neighbors' sheep, oblivious to the stress they might cause the ewes or lambs. Such antics were probably why the Danbys, whose sheep grazed in the fields around Cobble Hill, had added alpacas to their farm's menagerie. They made great security guards and didn't take any guff from mischievous dogs.

Harriet stomped into the barn where she found a couple posing for a selfie with Clyde, the donkey she had agreed to board while his owner recovered from hip surgery. "We prefer people not to disturb the animals in here, as some might be recovering from surgery or be in distress."

"We're not disturbing them," the woman insisted. "We're just taking pictures."

And how would you feel if I traipsed all over your property taking pictures? Harriet bit her tongue rather than ask the question aloud. "Your children just ran off somewhere," she told them.

"Oh dear," the woman exclaimed, and she and the man bustled after them.

Young Alfie emerged from the supply room with a scoop of feed for Clyde. "I tried to tell them to leave, but they didn't pay me any mind."

"I appreciate your efforts. I may have to consider locking the barn when we have animals convalescing or boarding."

"I could paint a big sign that says, 'Enter at your own risk.'"

Harriet laughed. "Tempting." She headed to the art gallery, happy to see that the pest control guys must have finished, since their truck was gone. She unlocked the back door and slipped inside.

The gallery brimmed with as many people as there were paintings. Harriet knew the crowds would thin out come winter. She would be grateful for them while they lasted. Art gallery dollars helped bridge the shortfall caused by inheritance tax and maintenance costs like their present squirrel infestation, not to mention skeptical farmers shying away from calling the new vet in town.

Her last telephone conversation with her mother careened through her thoughts. "Think positive, honey," she'd said. "Perhaps there's simply a sudden rash of good health among the county's animal population."

Harriet sidestepped a child dashing from the art room. Her grandfather had set aside a small back room for youngsters to explore their own creativity with water paints and crayons. If they wished, the children could then choose to display their art on the room's walls.

Mrs. Winslow spotted Harriet and waved her over. She'd told Harriet to call her Ida, but after years of knowing her as Mrs. Winslow,

Harriet had a hard time breaking the habit. The woman was in her midsixties, full of energy and enthusiasm. Her fine features and dark hair highlighted the hallmarks of her cheery disposition—endearing smile lines that creased her cheeks and the corners of her eyes.

"Can you believe all these people, love?" Mrs. Winslow tapped something on her phone and flipped it around for Harriet to see. "Look at the blog by the grandson of that fella who bequeathed your grandad's first painting to the gallery. It's had thousands of hits. You have an appointment with another reporter tomorrow morning. I checked with Polly and made sure you were free. Oh, and a national news program did a feature on your grandfather yesterday as part of their Yorkshire Day coverage. Isn't it wonderful?"

Harriet mirrored Ida's smile. "It's splendid." And it truly was.

But her helpless feeling over the sick calf preyed on her mind. She needed to dig through her grandfather's journals to see if he'd ever encountered anything like it. She also wanted to consult with a couple of the other local vets she'd met. The affliction could be unique to the area, but not common enough for Mr. Staveley to render his own diagnosis, as many of the local farmers were inclined to do.

"Do you need a hand?" Harriet asked Mrs. Winslow. "It's a madhouse in here."

"I have it well under control, dear." She twirled around to answer a visitor's question, clearly in her element.

Leaving the responsibility in Mrs. Winslow's capable hands, Harriet ducked out the way she'd come in and headed toward her office. Perhaps she should offer to host a get-together for their little group of area vets. They hadn't been able to match up their schedules in a while, what with busy work calendars and summer vacations.

She came across Charlie, who appeared to be stalking something in a bush along the path.

"What are you after?" Harriet asked her.

Charlie didn't spare her a glance. She poked her nose through the long grass, with one front paw raised, tail pointed straight back, looking for all the world as if she were imitating a pointer dog.

A mewling noise from the bushes heightened Harriet's senses. *Kittens?*

The sound came again, but it didn't sound like any kitten she'd ever heard. It sounded like—no, it was impossible.

She swept the bushes aside and found that she was right. It was a baby. Why on earth would someone abandon their infant here, in the bushes?

"Good boy, Charlie." Harriet covered the infant with the flannelette blanket on his lap to protect him from being scratched by branches then carefully drew his car seat out from under the bush. "Now, what are you doing here?" she asked, drawing off the blanket once more.

The child blinked at the sudden bright light then balled his hands and scrunched his face as if preparing to wail.

Harriet rocked the seat. "It's okay. Don't worry. We'll find your mom."

She was pretty sure this was the same baby who'd visited her clinic with his mother earlier. Which meant Aunt Jinny should know who his mother was—if the woman hadn't lied about having an appointment. She remembered the woman's furtive glances as she hurried across the grounds when Harriet left for the farm call.

Harriet beelined to the dower cottage, hoping Aunt Jinny was back. By the time she reached the clinic side of the cottage, the infant was bawling.

Jane Birtwhistle, a retired schoolteacher who took in every stray cat that passed by her cottage and was a regular vet client, emerged as Harriet reached the door. "Oh my. What's the matter with this little fellow?" She tickled the infant's tummy.

Before Harriet could inform her that she was searching for the child's mother, Jane foraged in the gap between the baby and his seat and then victoriously plunked a pacifier in the child's mouth. He sucked it eagerly, blessing them with instant silence.

Jane smiled at Harriet. "That did the trick."

The escalating tension drained from Harriet's neck and shoulders. "Thank you. I didn't even think to do that."

"My pleasure. This little one is much younger than the students I used to have to console in my teaching days, but the principle is always the same. If you can't address their felt need, distract them with something else. It's an approach that served me well for many years." She cocked her head. "Are you tending to babies as well as kitties now?"

"No, I believe this is one of my aunt's patients."

"That makes more sense. Let me get the door for you." Jane moved to the door and held it open.

Harriet thanked her again and hurried inside, where she saw Aunt Jinny's receptionist talking on the phone.

Aunt Jinny came into the waiting room, likely expecting the arrival of her next patient. When her gaze lit on Harriet and the baby, her eyes widened. "What have we here? Or rather, who?"

"I was hoping you could tell me."

Aunt Jinny's curious expression didn't give Harriet much confidence about the mother telling the truth with her doctor's appointment story.

"I found him under a bush outside."

"Abandoned? Goodness." Aunt Jinny felt the baby's forehead with the back of her hand and seemed satisfied he wasn't in urgent need of her attention. "Take him through to the kitchen and give me a few minutes." She turned to the receptionist, who had just concluded her phone call. "Moira, could you fetch Harriet a couple bottles of the infant formula samples that salesman left last week? And there should be spare nappies in the storage cupboard." Aunt Jinny winked at Harriet. "He might need a change after he's fed."

"Fed?" Harriet echoed. "I don't know how to feed a baby." She was an only child. She'd never even babysat as a teen. Dog-sat, sure. Even hamster-sat. But not babysat.

"Don't worry." Aunt Jinny's eyes twinkled with amusement. "It's not much different than bottle-feeding a lamb."

She followed Moira to the storage closet and asked, "Do you know who this baby belongs to? His mother popped into our office a few hours ago to use the bathroom. She said she had an appointment but Aunt Jinny was called out to an emergency."

"Oh, you must mean Rowena Talbot." Moira searched the shelves of the storage closet. "She's the only patient I wasn't able to reach who had an appointment scheduled for this afternoon." She tucked a couple of diapers under her arm and then collected two small bottles of prepared formula and two packaged bottle nipples. "Since she was our first appointment of the afternoon, we assumed she saw the note on the door and decided to reschedule Benji's appointment. How did he end up with you?"

Now Harriet remembered the young mother calling the baby Benji. "I found him under the bushes outside my clinic. Actually, Charlie, my cat, did. The mother apparently abandoned her son on my doorstep."

Moira stopped dead and spun on her heel, mouth agape.

The baby chose that moment to poke out his tongue, dislodging his pacifier, and instantly broke into a wail.

"Hey now, don't worry," Harriet soothed him, replacing the pacifier and bouncing his seat. "We'll find your mom."

Moira rushed to the clinic kitchen and started the kettle. "While this heats, let's get him out of that car seat and check him over."

Harriet's thoughts rioted at possible reasons for his frantic cries. "I have no idea how long he was under the bush." Besides being hungry or needing a change, he could be overheated or have been feasted on by any number of insects.

She set the car seat on the table and hurriedly unbuckled the harness to extract him.

Moira spread a fluffy bath towel over the washing machine and opened the nearby casement window to let in some fresh air. "Lay him on this and get him undressed while I fetch some baby wipes."

Harriet remembered thinking it was funny to see washing machines in the kitchen as a child when she visited Grandad. But the front-loading machine with its smooth top certainly came in handy for changing babies.

Her fingers fumbled over the snaps as Benji grew redder by the second. "It's okay, it's okay," she said over his cries, when it felt anything but okay to her either. Then remembering how she had calmed him earlier, she sang a lullaby as she eased his shirt over his head. He quieted once more but continued to scowl.

Moira returned with the promised baby wipes and popped the pacifier back into his mouth. "He likes your singing." She snatched the whistling kettle, poured the steaming water into a small bowl, and then set one of the bottles of formula into it. "We'll have this warmed up for you in no time," she told the boy in a singsong. To Harriet, she added, "Give me a second to run and check his file. Make sure he's not allergic to anything that we know of."

Harriet finished undressing him then scanned his unblemished skin as she continued to croon. When Moira came back, Harriet sang to her, "Doesn't look like he was bitten."

Smirking at Harriet's improv, Moira gave her a thumbs-up and sang back, "I didn't see any allergies or other issues in his records."

Benji gazed at the ceiling, appearing fascinated by the dark beams bisecting the white surface.

Moira blew on his belly, winning herself a giggle. "Now why would your mama leave an adorable little guy like you?" She scurried out of the room again, likely to check on the waiting room.

Harriet copied Moira and blew a raspberry on Benji's belly. "Whew." She abruptly drew back. "I've met cows that smelled sweeter. What's your mama been feeding you?" She wrinkled her nose at him. "I guess I could wash you while we wait for Moira." Placing one hand on Benji, Harriet attempted to reach the roll of paper towels sitting next to the farmhouse-style sink. Her fingers grazed the edge, but she couldn't quite grasp it.

Polly whirled in. "How's it going?"

"Can you hand me that roll of paper towels? What are you doing here?"

Handing over the requested roll, Polly gaped at the baby. "I stayed to finish July's invoices. When I left, I ran into Jane Birtwhistle, who told me you were taking care of a baby. What's going on?"

"I found him under the bushes, with Mom nowhere in sight. Actually, could you wet some of these with warm water for me?" Harriet handed back the paper towels.

"Sure thing." Polly glanced in her direction as she started the faucet. "I don't think I've ever seen you so uncomfortable. You're holding him like he's a bomb or something." She chuckled.

"This is not funny," Harriet scolded. "I don't have any experience with babies. Where is his mother?"

Moira hurried into the room. "I still can't reach his mum." She fastened a nipple onto the baby bottle and tested the temperature by sprinkling a few drops onto her wrist. "An automated message says she is 'currently unavailable.' I'm guessing that means her phone is out of range. I got her husband's voice mail though and left a message with him. So hopefully we'll hear back from one of them soon."

With Moira's guidance, Harriet managed to change Benji's diaper. With a little more fumbling, she even got him dressed again. Wiping her brow, Harriet wasn't sure who was more upset after the experience—him or her.

Polly scooped him up, cooing to him. "Can I feed him?"

"Fine by me." Harriet passed her the bottle Moira had prepared, but he didn't seem to want it. He fussed and turned his face away.

Polly frowned. "I don't think he likes me. What am I doing wrong?"

"It's not you," Moira assured her. "He's probably not used to drinking from a bottle."

"It might go better with someone we know he likes. You give it a go, Harriet." Polly handed the baby and bottle to her.

As soon as he was settled in Harriet's arms, Benji attacked the bottle with gusto.

Polly shook her head. "Okay, now I have a complex."

Moira chuckled. "Harriet's scent or feel might simply match his mother's more closely than yours."

"Eau de cow barn?" Harriet quipped, feeling absurdly pleased by how quickly he'd taken to the bottle for her.

Moira shook her head. "I think Rowena is a townie. Lives in a row house in White Church proper. Not sure what her husband does for his regular job, but I know he volunteers with RNLI."

"What's that?" Harriet asked.

"The Royal National Lifeboat Institution," Polly said. "A search-and-rescue service founded a couple hundred years ago to save lives at sea."

"Like the coast guard?"

"No, it's a separate entity operated almost entirely by volunteers, but it assists them sometimes."

"The RNLI is credited with saving over one hundred forty-four thousand lives since it began," Moira said.

"Wow, that's extraordinary." Harriet shook her head. "I can't believe I've never heard of it. Wait, are those the people who sailed across the English Channel in World War II to rescue the stranded soldiers at Dunkirk?"

"They were a part of that rescue effort, along with hundreds of people piloting their own pleasure boats, schooners, fishing boats, working barges—basically whatever could make the crossing," Moira explained, with obvious pride in how her country's people worked together to achieve such a heroic feat.

Benji started to fuss, and Harriet shifted him to her shoulder and began patting his back. "You want your daddy to come here and rescue you from the horrible ladies, don't you?" She turned her attention once again to Moira. "Is Aunt Jinny almost done with her patient? If you can't get ahold of Benji's parents, I think we should call the police."

Aunt Jinny rushed into the room. "No need to do that yet."

"Yeah," Polly agreed. Was she blushing? Van Worthington, the young detective constable in the village, clearly had a crush on Polly, who didn't seem to know how she felt about that.

"A woman has abandoned her child on my doorstep," Harriet reminded them. "If not for the fact that I was pretty sure he belonged to one of your patients, or at least someone who claimed to be his mother and a patient of yours, I would've already called the police. I mean, this is serious. What was the mother thinking?"

Aunt Jinny relieved Harriet of the little boy and laid him on the towel, where she listened to his chest with her stethoscope, checked his ears and eyes, and then took his temperature. Finally, she peeked at the back of his neck. "Yes, this is definitely Benji Talbot. I can tell by the birthmark on the nape of his neck. I'm reluctant to involve the police and the Department for Education, because doing so could create all kinds of ongoing problems for Rowena when she least needs them."

"What about her baby's needs?" Harriet pointed out. She assumed the Department for Education was the equivalent of Child Protective Services in the States.

"I'm certified as an emergency foster provider. If we involved the authorities, I would request permission to care for Benji until his parents are located anyway."

"Then that's what we should do."

"No, you don't understand." Aunt Jinny scooped up Benji once more. "Rowena has been suffering with the baby blues since giving birth. Postpartum depression. And with no family nearby to offer support and her husband frequently traveling for work, it's been an extra struggle for her."

"Aunt Jinny, she abandoned her baby," Harriet protested. "Isn't his welfare more important?"

"Yes, but as his doctor, I can assure you that he'll be better off if he can stay with his mum and she gets the support she needs. I've already called Pastor Will, and he's promised to enlist volunteers to make regular visits to Rowena and help her however she needs it. Maybe provide a meal or take this little guy for a walk in his pram so she can get a moment to herself."

"That's all well and good," Harriet said, knowing the thoughtful minister's heart was in the right place. Many days she wished she could grab a nap herself, so she couldn't imagine how much more intense that would be with a baby. "But where is Rowena now? And what happens the next time she feels overwhelmed and no one is around? If that's what happened today. I hate to think what could've happened to Benji if Charlie hadn't alerted me to his presence." She collapsed into a chair, and her aunt handed the baby to her.

"Is that why Charlie was going nuts outside just now?" Polly asked. "I had to pick her up so I could come inside and then set her back outside so she wouldn't trip me."

As if hearing her name, Charlie streaked into the room and made a beeline toward Harriet and Benji.

"Who let you in?" Polly asked the cat.

"My last patient must have as he was leaving," Aunt Jinny said. "She's fine. She's just checking on her charge."

Charlie stood on her hind legs against the chair that Harriet had settled in with Benji. She reached out a paw and gently touched the top of Benji's head.

"I think she fancies herself the little tyke's guardian angel," Moira said.

"That's so cute." Polly chuckled.

"Animals have a remarkable kinship when it comes to caring for young ones in need—even youngsters of other species," Harriet explained. "But regarding what to do about him, I really think I should alert the authorities to the situation. I feel for Rowena, but I still think we should go through the proper channels."

"I understand that," Aunt Jinny conceded, "and I already shared more about his mother's condition than I should have. But as her primary-care physician, as well as Benji's, I can assure you he'll come to no harm if we wait a little while. Whereas untold mental trauma could be foisted on his mother if we bring the authorities in now. After all, we don't know for sure that he has been abandoned. We don't know what happened to her. It won't hurt to keep Benji here while we look for her."

"I found him in the bushes with his mother nowhere to be seen. That seems like abandonment to me," Harriet said.

"Yes, but I can unofficially be Benji's foster parent until we hear from Rowena or her husband." Aunt Jinny lifted him from Harriet's arms. "I'll ask Pastor Will to drive by their house and see if Rowena has returned there."

"What reason do you think she had for leaving Benji, if you don't believe it was actual abandonment?" Harriet asked.

"She might have needed a few moments to herself if she was feeling overwhelmed. If he was sleeping, she could have decided to set him in the shade while she had a little walk around the farm. Come to think of it, she might have come back and found him gone, in which case she would be quite frantic."

"I have a friend who works dispatch at the police department," Moira chimed in. "I'll ask her to call us if they get a call about a missing infant. If she asks questions, I can remind her that patient privacy prevents me from sharing any details."

"I can scout the public footpaths around the farm," Polly volunteered. "See if I can find her. I'll get a few of my friends to help."

"That'd be great," Aunt Jinny said. "Are you okay with that, Harriet?"

Harriet glanced at the wall clock. "It's four now. I'm willing to give you until eight o'clock tomorrow morning. If we haven't found Rowena or heard from her husband by then, I think we have to call the police."

Aunt Jinny nodded. "Agreed."

Harriet prayed that delaying the call wouldn't prove to be a huge mistake.

CHAPTER FOUR

After eating a late supper, Harriet retreated to her grandfather's study, accompanied by Maxwell and Charlie, and tugged several years' worth of leather-bound journals from the floor-to-ceiling shelves. She made herself comfortable in her favorite cushioned armchair by the window and then scanned every entry for the month of August for several years. But she couldn't find a single incident of a cow exhibiting similar symptoms to Ned Staveley's calf.

Flicking a glance at the remaining years of journals, she rose and pressed her palms to her back. After finding Benji, she'd forgotten all about phoning her colleagues, Barry Tweedy, Gavin Witty, and Nigel Ellerby, for a get-together. She stretched her neck from side to side then picked up her cell phone and started composing a group text, outlining the symptoms. She didn't know how long it would take to organize an actual meeting, and she needed answers sooner rather than later.

Hearing what sounded like a mouse or possibly a squirrel scrabbling inside the wall, she set her phone down and slapped the plaster in the vicinity of the noise. "The pest guys were supposed to take care of you. Charlie," she called, no longer seeing her cat curled in the other chair. "You're slacking in your duties."

When Charlie didn't come running, Harriet peered out the window. The resourceful feline had probably finagled her way back into Aunt Jinny's place to keep watch over the baby.

Harriet grabbed a glass of water then decided to trek over herself to see how Benji was doing and find out if Aunt Jinny had heard from his parents yet. "Let's go, Maxwell. You can keep me company on the way over." Stepping outside, she saw a small group of people milling about in the field. Polly had said she'd get some of her friends to help look for Rowena, and this must be them.

She meandered toward the gate that opened into the pasture. Recognizing Polly and Will in the group, she waved.

Will headed her way, while Polly waved back and called that she'd see Harriet in the morning.

Harriet waited by the gate, shivering as goose bumps erupted on her arms when the handsome pastor approached.

"Hi," he said as he drew closer. "How are you holding up?"

She wrapped her arms around her torso. Emotion that she hadn't let herself acknowledge welled up at the concern in his hazel eyes. "I can't understand how Rowena could walk away from her baby. If that's what she did, is it wise to trust her with him when she returns? Or worse, what if we're wrong and she didn't abandon him? What if she's hurt and needs help?"

"We've searched the moors in every direction for the past few hours. No sign of her. I'm trying to reserve judgment until we actually know what happened. Right now, there's not enough information."

Harriet sighed. "I was on my way to Aunt Jinny's to see how she's doing with Benji. Care to join me?"

"Sure." He let himself through the gate. "I was thinking Rowena might have mentioned to Jinny the name of a friend or relative she might go to."

"If she did, don't you think that person would be moving heaven and earth to track down the baby?"

"Good point. Unless Rowena told them a story about leaving Benji with his dad or a babysitter."

They walked toward Aunt Jinny's, and Harriet noticed that Will tempered his long stride to match her shorter one. The silver threads in his brown hair belied his age, as he was only in his midthirties. But his physique was as lean as that of a younger man.

"How's work going? Are the old-timers warming up to you yet?" he asked, startling her from her musings.

"Some are, but others not so much. I encountered a mysterious case today—a calf exhibiting neurological symptoms indicative of poisoning, yet with no obvious source for it."

"Can't a blood test tell you what the poison is?"

"It might have—"

"If you could have convinced the farmer to pay for it," he guessed.

"You know your flock well. The trouble is that he doesn't want to pay if the vitamin injection does the trick. But in the meantime, the calf could get much worse, and the results might not come in time to help him."

Will nodded. "I hear you."

"It's so frustrating. If I lose the calf, chances are Mr. Staveley will never trust his animals to me again. He owns one of the largest farms in the area, and I'm concerned that his opinion will have a lot of influence on others."

"Well, I'd suggest you give it to him straight. Make it clear that a blood test is essential to an accurate diagnosis and that any further delay could cost him his calf and perhaps others. If he refuses to consent to the blood test, put the responsibility for the outcome squarely on his shoulders."

Harriet rubbed her arm. "In my head I know that's what I need to do. But in the moment, standing my ground doesn't always come so easily."

"Is that because you're worried about what the farmer will think of you?" His tone was reminiscent of the soothing one Aunt Jinny used with Benji.

"I guess."

"That's the problem. I know you care more about the animal's welfare than what Ned Staveley thinks of you. Make sure he knows it too. Then I daresay you'll win him over."

"You think so?"

"I do." Will's smile lit a fire in her soul and made her believe it was really that simple. "Farmers like Mr. Staveley respect people who care more about their work than their popularity."

"I'll try that. If the calf shows no sign of improvement in the morning, I'll insist on the blood test. Hopefully, it's a moot point, but I have a feeling it won't be."

Aunt Jinny stepped outside as they reached the porch. She carried Charlie, who looked rather indignant about being banned from the house. "Any luck finding Rowena?" she asked, setting Charlie down. The cat sauntered away, tail twitching in irritation.

"Sorry, there's no sign of her," Will said.

"Have you heard from her husband?" Harriet asked.

"Not yet. At least Benji went to sleep without a struggle. I imagine he'll be up to feed in the night once or twice and might not be so easy to console then."

"Call me if you need another pair of hands," Harriet volunteered. "I'm used to being called out at all hours."

"Thank you. I should be okay. I've hit that age where I'm often up myself at least once or twice a night."

Will chuckled. "Perhaps you and Benji can sync your internal clocks."

"Exactly."

"Well, my offer still stands," Harriet said.

"I appreciate it. I think I'll head to bed now myself to get a head start on sleeping. Then I shouldn't feel so tired if he has me up for a while."

"Could you text me to let me know if you hear from Rowena or Clive?" Will asked.

"Me too, please," Harriet added.

"Of course. I'll keep you both updated."

"I'll say good night then." Will stepped away from the porch with a wave.

Harriet walked him to his car. "Would you like to come in for a cup of tea or coffee or something cold before you head home?" He drove a black hearse that he'd acquired from a local funeral home at a cut-rate price, although if he had to visit a sick parishioner who might find the sight of a hearse pulling into their drive distressing, he'd borrow someone else's car. Tonight, Harriet wished he'd done that. The hearse's telltale appearance felt like a horrible omen.

"Thanks for the offer, but I'd better not stay. If I don't get started on my sermon prep tonight, I'll never be ready by Sunday."

Disappointment prickled. Probably from the realization that she'd been hoping to procrastinate getting back to her own work. That was all. There was no other reason for the feeling. Or so she told herself.

After seeing him off, she brewed herself a cup of tea and settled Maxwell into his bed then returned to her grandfather's study to see if any of the local vets had responded to her text. But when she picked up her phone, she realized that, thanks to the sounds in the wall, she'd never finished typing it, let alone sending it. Hating to interrupt their evenings so late, she turned her attention once again to her grandfather's journals, this time sitting at his desk.

The next thing she knew, she was waking up with one of the journals as a pillow, the room was dark, and her half-empty cup of tea was cold. *Terrific.* At this rate she'd never get any answers.

She probably should have started with the online databases or tried a few veterinary forums to see if anyone else was seeing similar symptoms crop up. She wasn't sure how popular such forums were with mixed-practice veterinarians who were usually too busy to fit any extras into their schedule. But she'd explored one as a student that had a number of retired vets on it who'd happily answered students' questions. She opened her laptop and posted a description of the calf's symptoms to a couple of online forums with the subject line: *Have you seen these symptoms in cattle?*

Next, she did an online search. But it didn't net any new results other than the things she already suspected. And as she'd told Will, without a blood test, all she could do was guess. She checked back on the forums, but there were no responses yet. Her fellow UK vets were probably already in bed, while her American counterparts were likely still working.

Harriet finished composing her text to Barry, Gavin, and Nigel, asking if any of them had seen similar symptoms in their practices, and made a mental note to send it in the morning. Hopefully, they'd have a better handle on the cause. She powered off her computer then selected a couple of her grandfather's textbooks to thumb through in bed. Padding to the kitchen to dump her cold tea, she noticed the upstairs light was on at Aunt Jinny's. Must be Benji's midnight feeding. With any luck, it would carry the little guy through to daybreak.

Stifling a yawn, Harriet headed upstairs to bed with her textbooks and soon drifted off to sleep.

In the wee hours of Saturday morning, her phone blared.

Reaching for it, Harriet squinted at the clock. It was 4:33 a.m. "Cobble Hill Veterinary," she answered, mentally preparing herself to get up. Farmers rose with the sun, and while some tended to wait far too long before calling in a vet, others saw no point in waiting and risking her being called out somewhere else and unable to get to their animals for hours.

"Ned Staveley here. I got two more sick cows."

Harriet jumped out of bed and rushed to gather her clothes. "Same symptoms as the calf?"

"Yes, and he's getting worse."

"I'm on my way."

Although the sun hadn't risen above the horizon, the sky was already light. Harriet slid into the Beast and barreled out of the driveway.

The sight of a small blue compact car parked on the side of the road twenty yards from her driveway sent a shiver down her spine. Could it be Rowena's?

Harriet pulled in behind the car and, after jumping out of her truck, quickly scanned the car's interior. Finding it empty, she breathed a sigh of relief. Not that she hadn't hoped to find Rowena. She feared *how* she'd find her. Wanting to trust Aunt Jinny's character assessment, Harriet had begun to suspect that only something awful could have kept Rowena from returning for Benji.

Harriet jumped back into her truck and headed for Goose Beck Farm while voice-commanding her phone to call Aunt Jinny.

Her aunt picked up on the third ring, sounding groggy. "Harriet? Is everything all right?"

"Sorry to wake you, but I'm heading to a call and spotted a sky-blue Renault parked on the road." Harriet recited the license plate number. "Any chance it belongs to Rowena?"

"Oh dear. I think she does drive a blue Renault, though I'm not sure what her plate number is."

"It never occurred to me to check the road for abandoned cars. I assumed she would have parked outside your office."

"I've had several patients complain about art gallery visitors clogging the driveway," Aunt Jinny said.

"I'm sorry. I don't know what to do about that. And it's bound to get worse with the unveiling of Grandad's returned painting next weekend."

"I suppose you could always open the front field for parking. It's relatively flat. And with how dry the summer has been, no one should get stuck."

"Good idea. But Rowena was here before it got crowded. If this is Rowena's car, chances are something's happened to her."

Crying erupted in the background, as if Benji had heard her and somehow understood what she'd said.

"Sorry, I need to go," Aunt Jinny said. "Feeding time. But don't worry. I'll call the police about the car."

Harriet's stomach now had two reasons to churn. She should have insisted on taking the calf's blood yesterday, and she should have followed her instincts and called the police after not finding Rowena at Aunt Jinny's office.

As Will had said, she had to prioritize her patients' welfare first and foremost. Specifically, the calf's and Benji's, not Ned Staveley's and Rowena's. Although in Rowena's case, calling the police might have been the best for all concerned. There was no telling what might have occurred in the hours that had elapsed since Benji was found.

CHAPTER FIVE

As Harriet neared the Staveley farm, her heart sank. Few things were worse than having to put a herd under quarantine. And at the sight of Mr. Staveley and his grandchildren leading not two but three cows in from the field, fear gripped her that that was exactly where they were headed.

She scrutinized the animals' listing gaits. From her grandfather's descriptions of a mad cow disease outbreak he'd once dealt with, this could be a cousin to the disease, but she still felt it was more likely to be a case of poisoning.

The instant Mr. Staveley reached the barnyard, he locked the cattle in a small pen, his expression grim.

Harriet bit her tongue, determined to examine each cow thoroughly before saying what she suspected the man already knew. The cattle exhibited definite signs of poisoning, but it was their apparent blindness that made her strongly suspect lead poisoning in particular. Although she'd often wondered how well Highland cattle could see through the heavy fringe of hair, known as a dossan, that hung in front of their eyes. But she couldn't figure out how they could have managed to get into something containing lead on the moorlands. There weren't any old tractor batteries or scraps of painted wood or barrels of sump oil rotting out on the hills.

"I know we wanted to avoid this step, but at this point, I have to take blood tests." She prepared a syringe and vials. The decision was not up for debate, and Mr. Staveley knew it. She collected the samples and stowed them safely in her vehicle, deciding to drive them directly to the courier depot so they'd get to the lab before it closed and thereby be further ahead in the queue come Monday.

"Do you or your family consume milk from these cows?" Harriet asked. Highland cows were raised primarily for their meat, which was known for being lower in cholesterol. But while they didn't produce nearly as much milk as traditional dairy cows, their milk was rich in butterfat, making it a great choice for butter, cheese, and gelato.

"Sometimes."

"Recently?"

Mr. Staveley frowned. "Are you saying we shouldn't?"

"Have any of you felt poorly afterward?"

He crossed his arms defensively. "We wouldn't use milk from sick cows."

She nodded encouragingly, needing to ask the questions even if they made him uncomfortable. "That's good. And have these cows all been grazing exclusively on common land on the moors?"

"That's right."

"Along with any other herds?"

"Folds," he corrected. "A group of Highland cows is named after the open structure they can be kept in through the winter. And yes, there's another fold."

"How many are still out there?"

"Fifty of mine. A couple hundred of Gilbert Vail's."

"We'll need to quarantine them all." She'd have to stop by Gilbert Vail's farm so she could advise him to do the same.

"Is there nothing you can do?" Worry, not anger, vibrated through Mr. Staveley's words.

"Until we get the lab results, the best I can do is treat the symptoms, I'm afraid."

"You heard the doc," he said to his grandsons. "Go fetch the rest of the cows from the field."

They raced away, and the little girl started after them.

"Where do you think you're going, Abby?" her grandfather asked her.

"To see the bunnies."

The man's expression softened. "You can't wander out in those fields now, duck."

"Why not?" Abby protested. She couldn't have been more than seven or eight, and Harriet was surprised the child wasn't still snug in her bed at this early hour.

Mr. Staveley looked at Harriet helplessly. Harriet squatted down to the girl's level. "Because until we figure out what's making the cows sick, your grandad's farm is under quarantine, which means everyone has to stay put. We can't risk you or anyone else bringing germs in or out of the common fields."

Abby frowned and crossed her arms. "Bunnies aren't going to make the cows sick."

"No, but if you scare the mother rabbit, she might abandon her babies." Harriet's throat dried, thinking of the abandoned infant she'd discovered the day before.

"Are you the vet?"

"Yes."

"Did the lady find her cat?"

Harriet tilted her head. "What lady is that?"

Abby shrugged. "Dunno. I just heard a lady say her cat ran into the bushes at the vet's."

"Well, since none of my clients have asked me to be on the look-out for their missing cat, I'm sure she must've found it again."

"That's good."

"Off with you now," Mr. Staveley said, patting the little girl's head. "And mind how you go."

"I will," she responded with an unhappy sigh over her new boundaries.

"What about the public footpath?" he asked Harriet once Abby had wandered off. "This time of year, we get dozens of ramblers walking through every day."

Another possible vector for the disease or source of contamination she hadn't considered. "I have quarantine signs in my truck that can be posted at the gates to alert people. I'll put them up before I leave."

Mr. Staveley nodded, his face grim.

As Harriet drove away from the farm, she spotted Abby gazing forlornly over the stone wall that separated her grandfather's farm from the common land.

A lone, ramshackle stone barn of a bygone era stood in the next field, but no cattle were around it that Harriet could see. A wooden gate wide enough for a tractor, held together in places with twine, marked the entrance to the field. Fresh tracks indicated someone had recently driven in, reminding her she needed to call on the other farmer whose cattle also grazed the common land. She wasn't looking forward to the unpleasant response the news was destined to earn her. But he'd thank her later if the measures didn't prove to be too little too late.

She eased around a couple of construction workers in bright orange vests as they guided the driver of a skid loader off a flatbed truck. *What on earth are they working on now?* All summer she'd been confounded by diversion after diversion due to roadwork. And when roads were as few and far between as they were in the moors, detours could add hours to a day of farm visits.

Thankfully, her first appointment back at the clinic wasn't scheduled until ten thirty. Even better, she found Gilbert Vail surprisingly amiable, given the news she'd brought him. He was quite a bit younger than Ned Staveley, and insisted being on a first-name basis with Harriet. From all appearances, his farm would be fine. His impressive stone house draped in a second flush of purple wisteria sat at the top of a hill at the end of a tree-lined drive.

That taken care of, Harriet swung by the courier depot to drop off the blood samples, grateful they opened early. When she returned to her truck, she took a moment to send the text to the local vets. A glance at the dashboard clock told her she should arrive home with more than an hour to spare before clinic hours. Enough time to grab a quick shower and breakfast then check in with Aunt Jinny on Benji's status and that of the car's owner.

But by the time she reached Cobble Hill, the blue car was gone. Had it merely belonged to an early morning hiker? On her way up the driveway, she spotted a police car parked outside Aunt Jinny's place, and Harriet's heart clenched.

She parked hurriedly, dashed to the dower cottage, and pushed through the door without knocking. "What happened?"

Aunt Jinny appeared, bouncing Benji on her shoulder. "The car was Rowena's, as you feared."

"But it's gone. What happened to it?"

Detective Constable Van Worthington, a fair-skinned, blond-haired young man, answered. "I had it towed to headquarters in York so a forensics team can go over it."

"Oh wow. That's good, I suppose." Given that Rowena hadn't even been missing twenty-four hours yet, Van's response renewed Harriet's hope of a happy ending for Benji. "Have you been able to reach Benji's father?"

"No," Aunt Jinny said. "He must be traveling outside the country for work."

Van jotted a note onto his pad. "I'll check with passport control."

Benji reached toward Harriet, and her heart softened. Gently lifting him from her aunt's arms, she murmured, "It's okay, baby. We'll find your parents. I promise."

He buried his face in her shoulder.

"He's a good baby," Van commented. "He's clearly happy to be here. No wonder the director had no qualms about leaving him in your aunt's care until his parents are located."

"That was a quick decision," Harriet said. "Don't they usually send out a social worker?"

"Dispatch contacted the proper authorities as soon as the call came in. They notified me of their decision to leave Benji in Jinny's care before I even reached the farm."

"That's unusual, isn't it?"

The detective constable shrugged. "She's an approved foster provider. They probably couldn't think of anyone better to care for him than a doctor who's also a mother."

"And this way he's not put through any more trauma than he's already been through." Harriet laid her cheek on his head. "You hear that, Benji? You get to stay with us a while longer. Isn't that nice?"

He cooed at her as if in agreement.

Someone pounded on the door. "Jinny? Harriet?" Polly called.

Aunt Jinny opened the door, and Polly rushed in. "What happened? What are the police doing here?" Her gaze met the young DC's. "Hi, Van."

Van's ears reddened, and he cleared his throat. "Dr. Bailey found Rowena's car abandoned on the road."

"When we headed home after searching the moors last night, three cars were still here. I assumed they belonged to hikers." Polly sounded distraught. "It never occurred to me that one of the cars could've been Rowena's. If I'd thought to report it then, we might be closer to the truth now."

"It didn't occur to any of us," Aunt Jinny said. "Don't blame yourself."

"It makes sense for one of us to have thought of it," Harriet said. "If she'd wandered off onto the moors, of course her car would still be here."

"I don't know," Van chimed in. "What if she had walked here? You wouldn't have been looking for her car. Your place isn't far from town, especially by the cliffside trail. I imagine a fair share of your clients walk here, don't they?"

"Not carrying their baby in a car seat," Polly pointed out.

Harriet's phone rang.

Stifling a groan, she handed Benji back to Aunt Jinny and sent a prayer skyward that she'd have time to grab herself breakfast before whatever emergency was coming in now.

She sagged in relief at the sight of Mrs. Winslow's number on the phone screen. "Good morning. What's up?"

"Reporter's here."

"How did he even find out?" Aunt Jinny asked, apparently overhearing Mrs. Winslow's announcement. "He's bound to twist everything to sensationalize this as abandonment and make Rowena out to be an unfit mother, all in a bid to sell newspapers."

"Not at all," Harriet soothed. "The reporter is here to see me about the unveiling of Grandad's painting. He scheduled the appointment yesterday."

Aunt Jinny clutched Benji to her chest and shrank from the view of the window. "Well, please don't mention anything about finding the baby."

"Why?" Polly asked. "I mean, I understand your concern that he might demonize Rowena, but if she got lost walking and we get the word out, the public could help us find her." Polly turned to Van. "Wouldn't you agree?"

A blush swept up his neck and into his cheeks once more. "Maybe I should check with DI McCormick before you mention anything to the reporter." He withdrew his cell phone from his utility belt and made the call. Detective Inspector Kerry McCormick, from county headquarters, often consulted on crimes beyond what White Church Bay's department was equipped to handle.

Harriet grew antsy about keeping the reporter waiting. "I need to go," she mouthed to Van as he explained the situation to his superior. The gallery opened at ten o'clock, which gave her twenty-five minutes to give the reporter an interview and a private tour. And Polly needed to be back in the clinic and behind the receptionist's desk.

Van held up one finger to signal her to wait. "Yes, I understand. Will do," he said into his phone before disconnecting. "DI McCormick is adamant that word of the baby's abandonment not be leaked to anyone. She wants our office to control the narrative."

Polly propped her hands on her hips. "It's a bit late for that, wouldn't you say? I already had half a dozen of my mates here last night helping me search for Rowena. And the pastor probably put her on the prayer chain."

"No," Aunt Jinny said. "I asked him to keep the search quiet for Rowena's sake. You told your friends not to put on social media what they'd been up to like I asked, right?"

"Yes, but that doesn't mean they didn't blab about it to their families or flatmates when they got home."

"Okay, well. I can't keep the reporter waiting any longer," Harriet said. "I won't breathe a word about the baby."

Her grandfather had managed to create enough of a following all on his own. She didn't need a salacious story to catapult Cobble Hill's reputation into the zone of notoriety to draw more visitors to the gallery. In fact, with how much she'd been tripping over them lately, she might regret agreeing to the interview at all.

CHAPTER SIX

Harriet slipped through the gallery's main entrance and locked it behind her, hoping she hadn't attracted the attention of the visitors already milling about the farm, or they'd be queuing at the door.

A man in his midforties, wearing a collared shirt and jeans as rumpled as his hair, strode toward her with one hand extended, the other steadying the camera hanging from his neck. "I'm Fraser Kemp. You must be Doc Bailey's granddaughter."

"Yes, Harriet Bailey."

"Right. 'One day, my Harriet's going to take over this place,' he used to say. He all but burst with pride when he heard you decided to train to be a vet."

Harriet's heart swelled with love and more than a little melancholy that she hadn't made it back to the UK to visit Grandad as often as she would've liked in the past few years.

"You were friends with my grandfather?"

"Everyone was. Whenever he dropped by the pub, someone would offer to buy him a pint. Mind you, he always opted for a fizzy drink instead. He wanted to stay sharp. 'Never know when an emergency might come in,' he used to say. But that didn't stop him from joining with the lads at the pub for quiz night or a round of darts now and again."

Harriet smiled at the image the man's words conjured in her mind. Her grandad had taught her to play darts and then been awed by the fact that she inevitably scored two to three bull's-eyes a game. She'd thought he was throwing the game to boost her confidence until she realized most players couldn't manage to score a single bull's-eye.

She shook the reminiscing from her head. She'd soon have a clinic full of patients waiting for her, and she needed to get through this interview.

"You've definitely fixed up the art gallery since I was last here. It looks great."

"Thank you, Mr. Kemp."

"Call me Fraser."

"All right. Where would you like to start, Fraser? It sounds as if you probably know more about my grandfather's history than I do."

"Yes, I can easily handle that section of the article. How about you show me this new piece you recently discovered?"

"Yes, follow me." She led the way to the back room. "An art student our pastor connected me with, Stu Nelson, just finished restoring the piece to its original luster. But he can only come in on weekends. That's why I'm holding off the unveiling until next weekend."

"Where did you find the painting?"

Harriet fiddled with the doorknob, but it refused to turn under her hand. "Sorry, this knob seems to be temperamental today." She grunted as she put her shoulder to the door. "The painting was bequeathed to the gallery from the Henderson estate." She rattled the doorknob without success.

"Here, let me." Fraser withdrew a small spray bottle from his camera bag. He carefully sprayed around the doorknob then wiggled it. A moment later, the door magically opened. "I never leave home without this. It's dry lubricant. You never know when you'll need it." He tucked the spray bottle back into his bag.

"Thank you." She flicked on the overhead light. "As I was saying, Mr. Henderson was a fourth-generation Yorkshire farmer and very young when my grandad saved what eventually grew to be his dad's prize bull. Grandad was already dabbling in painting and created a portrait of the calf taking his first unsteady steps." Harriet wandered about the room, shifting drop cloths in an effort to discover where the piece had gotten to. "Grandad called it 'The First Unsteady Steps to Greatness.'"

"How fitting that it was true not only of the bull in the painting but also of your grandad's work as a veterinarian and an artist."

"That's exactly what the farmer said in his will and why he wanted it returned to the official Bailey collection, since neither his daughter nor his grandson were interested in taking over the farm. We plan to make limited-edition prints available for purchase and will gift one to his daughter. Excuse me a minute."

Harriet stepped out of the room and called for the gallery manager. "Mrs. Winslow, did Stu tell you where he left the painting he's been working on? The Henderson painting?" To Fraser, she added, "It had gotten a bit grimy hanging in the farmer's old stone cottage for the past fifty years, as you can well imagine."

"It's on the easel in the corner with a drop cloth over it." Mrs. Winslow bustled over and preceded Harriet back into the room.

At her gasp and the sight of the empty easel, Harriet's heart sank like a rock. She already had enough on her plate trying to establish herself as a reputable vet in the area. Not that she'd expected to be able to just sweep in on her grandfather's coattails and carry on where he'd left off, but the task had proven more difficult than she'd anticipated. Between finding an abandoned baby on her doorstep, dealing with a mysterious ailment of possibly epidemic proportions among the Staveley cattle, and now this, she didn't think she could take much more. She wanted to sit down and cry.

"It was there yesterday morning," Mrs. Winslow insisted. "I saw it."

"Do you think it's been stolen?" Fraser's voice was too animated as he snapped a picture of the empty easel.

"Wait," Harriet said. "What are you doing? We don't know that it's been stolen."

Fraser whipped out his pad and pen and scribbled on it. "You say you last saw it yesterday morning?" he asked Mrs. Winslow, who went into minute detail of the day, including the fact she'd had to open the door to the room to allow the exterminators access to the attic hatch.

"*Pest control*," Harriet corrected, envisioning animal-rights protesters descending on the place next. "They weren't exterminating anything."

"So these pest control guys would've been the last ones to see the painting before it was nicked," Fraser said.

"Or *they* nicked it." Mrs. Winslow worriedly patted her chest.

"Don't touch anything," Harriet ordered, finally coming to her senses. "I'll fetch DC Worthington."

If Fraser thought it strange that she identified a specific officer instead of saying she'd call the police, he didn't comment.

As she hurried to the door, she could only pray he wouldn't ask what Van was doing here already. Spotting the queue of visitors that had already formed outside the gallery entrance, she retreated out of sight and phoned Polly.

"Is Van still here?" she asked the instant Polly picked up.

"I left him with Jinny. I had to open the clinic. Wait. I see him heading to his car now."

"Get out there and stop him," Harriet said. "My grandfather's Henderson painting has gone missing."

"Yikes. All right. I'm on it." Polly kept the line open, and Harriet heard her run out of the clinic and call, "Van! Harriet is on the phone for you."

In a few seconds she heard Van say, "I've got it." Then, into the phone, he asked, "What's wrong?"

Harriet relayed their discovery. "And there's a line of people waiting to come into the gallery. What should I do?"

"Is there any evidence of a break-in?"

"No. If I hadn't had the appointment with the reporter this morning, we wouldn't have been any the wiser until we set up for the unveiling." She winced at the possibility of having to cancel it.

"Okay, I'll be right there. Tell people the gallery will open a little late." Van disconnected.

Harriet snatched up a stack of the gallery's business cards and summoned Mrs. Winslow as she hurried to the front door to admit Van. To the people already in line at the door, she said, "Thank you for your patience. Due to unforeseen circumstances, today's opening must be delayed. Mrs. Winslow will give each of you a voucher for 10 percent off any gift shop purchase if you wish to wait or return later."

Van arrived, and Harriet handed Mrs. Winslow the stack of business cards and asked her to note on the back of each one that it was good for a special discount.

Mrs. Winslow faced the group. "If you'd like to gather at the tables and benches in the garden next to the gallery, I can make us all a spot of tea. I have a few stories of Doc Bailey's vet days that I can regale you with."

The offer earned a hearty cheer.

Leaving the visitors in Mrs. Winslow's capable hands, Harriet ushered Van inside, ignoring the questions about why the police were there and praying Mrs. Winslow would be discreet.

"It appears we may have had a security breach," she heard Mrs. Winslow saying. "The detective constable has kindly come to see that Doc Bailey's beloved paintings remain secure."

"She's good," Van said to Harriet after she locked the door behind them.

"Yes, a real gem." Movement in the corner of the room caught Harriet's attention.

What was Fraser doing over there?

"I thought I'd make a few notes about other pieces in the gallery while I waited," he explained.

She had more or less abandoned him. "I'm sorry. I suppose we might as well postpone the interview, since there won't be an unveiling until we recover the missing painting."

"I'd like to stay, if you don't mind. I rarely get to cover the crime beat."

Harriet winced at his enthusiastic tone. "I'm not sure this is the kind of story I want published."

"Might give other thieves ideas," Van said.

Harriet hadn't even considered that possibility. "Please don't report on this, Fraser." Between finding Benji's parents and figuring out what made the Staveleys' cows sick, she had enough to worry about without adding security upgrades to her to-do list.

"Who knew the painting was here?" Van asked her.

"A recent blog post about it went viral, and it was also covered on TV, so I can't say for sure how many others knew about it. Although the public wouldn't have known where it was stored. Besides me, only Aunt Jinny, Polly, Mrs. Winslow, and Stu Nelson, the art student who worked on its restoration, knew it was in the back room."

"Except for your exterminators," Fraser reminded her.

"True. Rhys and Ronnie from Reynolds Pest Control were in here yesterday to deal with a gray squirrel infestation. They would have accessed the attic through that room."

"Was the painting still here after they left?"

"I couldn't say. We'd have to ask Mrs. Winslow."

"When was anyone else in here recently that you know of?"

"Stu completed the restoration work on Thursday."

They went into the back room, and Van examined the lead-paned window then pulled down the ladder connected to the attic hatch. He climbed up and aimed his flashlight beam around. After a minute or two, he descended the ladder and closed the hatch then checked all the gallery windows. "There's no evidence that any of the windows were forced. It seems likely that whoever took the painting walked straight in and out the main door."

"Isn't there a back door?" Fraser asked.

"There is." Harriet showed it to Van, but it didn't appear to have been forced open either.

"We could be looking at a simple snatch-and-run or something more sophisticated involving a thief capable of picking a lock," Van said, making notes. "Is anything else missing?"

Harriet scanned the walls and didn't detect any gaps among the displayed paintings. "Not that I can tell."

"Could be an inside job," Fraser speculated.

Harriet gaped at him. "No way. Mrs. Winslow is no thief."

Fraser held up his hands in surrender. "It was a theory. I should get going."

Harriet deflated. "Yes, of course. I'll let you out."

To Van, Fraser added, "Be sure to get the painting listed on the Art Loss Register. Reputable dealers check it before acquiring valuable paintings."

"Thanks for the tip," Van said. Then he turned to Harriet. "You might as well let the visitors in now, but keep the door to the back room locked. I'll see about dusting for fingerprints after I ask Mrs. Winslow a few questions."

By the time Harriet opened the door for Fraser, the waiting crowd had doubled in size. Harriet motioned them inside. "Come on in."

The group was the most animated of any she'd ever seen. Whatever stories Mrs. Winslow had shared must have really cranked up their interest.

Van drew Mrs. Winslow aside to ask his questions.

A text from Polly reminded Harriet that her first appointment was scheduled to begin in fifteen minutes. "Van, if you don't need me for anything else, I should get back to the clinic."

"I'll walk you over there." Van asked Mrs. Winslow a couple more questions and jotted her answers in his notebook, including that she couldn't confirm the painting was still in the room after the Reynolds brothers left. Although she insisted that she'd known "the boys" since they were knee-high and they would never do something like that.

"If you think of anything else, give me a call," Van told her.

Harriet's legs felt like cement blocks as she and Van headed out. "Be honest with me. What are the chances of recovering my grandfather's painting?"

"Not great, I'm afraid."

Aunt Jinny hurried toward them, pushing Benji in a stroller with Charlie in hot pursuit. "Any leads on where Rowena is?"

"No." Needing to steady her nerves, Harriet scooped up Charlie and hugged her. The cat's purr was soothing. "We think one of Grandad's paintings has been stolen."

As Harriet detailed the unhappy discovery, Polly joined them in the parking lot. "What if Rowena was the one who took it?"

"That's ridiculous," Aunt Jinny said. "She wouldn't abandon her child in the hopes of making a few quid off a painting."

"It's worth more than that," Harriet corrected, setting Charlie back on the ground.

"But the doc's right," Van said. "And anyway, don't forget, Rowena left without her car. With all the people here yesterday, surely someone would have noticed her walking away with a painting."

"She could've had an accomplice," Polly speculated. "Maybe she had a getaway car waiting."

"She wouldn't have left her baby," Aunt Jinny said again.

Charlie twined around Aunt Jinny's legs, whining as if to show her solidarity.

"But you said yourself she'd been feeling down since his birth," Polly reminded her.

Aunt Jinny glared at Polly, her gaze momentarily flicking to Van.

Harriet understood her feeling uncomfortable with Polly blurting out Rowena's private struggles. But given these new developments, Van needed to be aware of the young mother's potential state of mind.

Especially if the effects were beginning to reach beyond Rowena herself.

CHAPTER SEVEN

Harriet's thoughts rioted as her gaze drifted from the building that housed the art gallery to the cars lining the drive and then to the pastures. "Would a new mother really abandon her baby to snatch a painting?"

"No, she wouldn't," Aunt Jinny said in a tone that suggested she was tired of saying it but would continue to do so until others believed as she did.

Benji burst into tears at her stern voice, and Harriet scooped him into her arms. Rocking him gently, she whispered reassurances in his ear, surprised by how natural the reaction felt.

Charlie immediately left Aunt Jinny's side to twine around Harriet's legs.

Polly picked Charlie up. "Benji's okay, see?"

Charlie gently tapped a paw on Benji's shoulder as if needing to reassure herself. The attention immediately stopped Benji's sniffles.

Meanwhile, Aunt Jinny fixed her glare on Van. "Rowena wouldn't abandon her child to score some easy money."

Sensing Benji about to fuss again, Harriet smiled and bounced him, saying in a singsong, "No one is saying your mama is a thief. We just have to consider all the possibilities." She snuggled him closer, inhaling his sweet scent and trying not to think about how much she'd always looked forward to having a baby after she was married. Aunt Jinny was already a mother at Harriet's age, and yet Harriet herself seemed further away from motherhood than ever.

A lime-green Citroen rolled up the driveway, and Will waved from the passenger window as the driver parked nearby.

Distant church bells rang the half hour, and Harriet realized she was late for her first appointment. Passing Benji back to her aunt, she asked Polly to let their waiting clients know she'd be right in. Then she said to Van, "There's another possibility."

Polly's steps faltered.

"Rowena could have witnessed the robbery," Harriet said. "Realizing the thief saw her, perhaps she hid Benji in the bushes for his protection then dashed off to hide herself, leading the danger away from her child." It sounded so much nobler than believing the mother would abandon her infant son. And for Benji's sake, Harriet really wanted to believe it was true.

"But if the thief caught up to her?" Polly asked. Harriet didn't want to contemplate what the thief might have done to ensure her silence.

"Either way," Van said as Will jumped out of the strange car and dashed around to the hatchback, "that would mean that if we find the thief, we'll find the painting and the baby's mother."

Will scooped something from the back of the car that was wrapped in an old blanket. "I didn't know where to bring it." He hurried toward them, cradling his cargo against his chest. A gangly leg slipped from his hold.

"A fawn?" Harriet blurted. "Where did you find it? Is it hurt?"

"Orphaned."

"Are you sure? Mother deer can leave their young for ten to twelve hours while they forage."

Harriet edged back the blanket. The fawn's coat appeared healthy, which reinforced her doubts that it had truly been orphaned. And now, instead of an abandoned baby, they had a bereaved mama wandering around the woods.

"I'm sure." Will flinched. "I struck its mother with my car. She dashed into the lane as I rounded the bend. I swerved, but so did she, and there was nothing I could do." His gaze dropped to the fawn in his arms. "The mama managed to keep moving a few more yards before collapsing near this little fellow. It was almost as if she led me to him."

Harriet's heart shifted at the anguish in his voice. "I'll be glad to look at him if you don't mind waiting for a bit. I have a couple of other clients ahead of you, and then we can check him over properly. You might need to bottle-feed him for a few weeks." She let the blanket drop back over the fawn. "It's a roe deer, which are always small, so it might be older than it looks. They're usually born in May and June. If he was born in May, then he'll have no trouble with foraging. If he's a June baby, he might not be quite ready to make it on his own."

"Whatever I have to do, I will. I feel terrible about this."

Harriet smiled. She knew he was kind and friendly to each person he met, but clearly, he cared deeply for the welfare of all God's creatures.

As he followed her into the clinic, he asked, "Is Van here with news about Rowena?"

"I'll catch you up after I care for my morning patients, okay?"

He nodded. "I'm sorry for holding you up."

"Not at all. Since that didn't look like a local who dropped you off, I'm sure you made your own sacrifices to get here."

"I called a tow truck for the hearse, which I'm afraid is ready for its own funeral. But when a passerby stopped and offered his help, I figured the sooner I could get this little guy here, the better."

When Harriet entered the clinic, Polly handed her the file on their first patient, who was already waiting in an exam room. By half past twelve, she'd tended three dogs, one rabbit, the fawn, and a litter of kittens.

Stretching the kinks from her back, she joined Polly at the reception desk. "What's next?"

Polly tapped a few keys on her keyboard. "I've sent you the address for Martha Banks, who runs a hobby farm nearby where she rehabilitates injured wildlife. I've already called her, so I thought you might want to take Pastor Will there with the fawn. Martha would probably be willing to take him off the pastor's hands."

"He's still here?"

"He has no vehicle, remember? I told him you'd likely be able to drop him off wherever he needed to go when you went out for your afternoon calls."

"Do I have any besides Martha?"

"No." She smirked. "But I didn't think you'd mind chauffeuring the pastor."

Harriet didn't rise to the bait. "Not at all. But I do need to do more research on what could be afflicting Mr. Staveley's cows. That reminds me." She snatched her phone from her pocket. "I haven't had time to see if any of the local vets responded to my text on the Staveley case."

"I checked the vet boards you posted to last night, but the replies basically echoed your theory. I also called three other farm vets in the North York Moors. None have seen any cattle or other animals exhibiting the symptoms you're seeing."

"Okay. Thanks for doing that for me." Scrolling through the equally unhelpful responses from Barry, Gavin, and Nigel, she sighed. "Hopefully, I still might find something useful in my grandfather's journals. If I ever get a chance to go through more of them."

"I'm happy to stay an extra couple of hours and skim through a few for you," Polly offered. "Between finding Benji and now the theft, you've got more than enough balls to juggle."

"Are you gunning for a raise?" Harriet teased.

Polly winked. "I wouldn't refuse one."

Harriet found Will with Aunt Jinny, enjoying the shade of a big tree next to the pasture. Benji and Charlie entertained each other while the fawn drank eagerly from the bottle Will held. "Quite the interesting group we have here," Harriet said.

Aunt Jinny laughed. "I watch Charlie around Benji of course, but they clearly adore each other. And Will is getting the hang of being a foster parent too."

Harriet smiled at Will, whose cheeks flushed at the compliment.

"I need to make a couple of house calls this afternoon and check on a patient recovering in the hospital," Aunt Jinny added. "Polly told me you don't have any clinic appointments this afternoon. Would you be able to take care of Benji while I'm gone? Will said he'd be happy to join you on your calls to help with him."

"Sure. Though I don't have any official calls at the moment. I do need to see Martha Banks about taking in the fawn, and I'd like to take a closer look at the fields where the Staveley cattle have been grazing."

"That's good. The drive should lull Benji to sleep, and I'll send some supplies with you for him." She nudged Will. "This one will be an expert at bottle-feeding by the end of the day."

"Jinny told me about your grandfather's painting going missing, likely stolen," Will said. "I was sorry to hear about that."

"I would have told you myself when I examined the fawn, but I didn't think of it. I was rushed off my feet this morning."

"I understand. Is there anything I can do to help?"

"Help me track down the crook?" Harriet suggested, half joking.

"Sure," he said without hesitation. "If I can."

"I'm not sure how DI McCormick will feel about us poking around," Aunt Jinny said. "She hasn't been too happy about it in the past."

"So we'll keep it to ourselves," Harriet replied. "I'm sure Van would be happy to run with any leads we send his way."

"How much more do you think he'll have to do with the cases now that DI McCormick has taken over?" Aunt Jinny asked.

"With how tight the police budget is," Will said, "I think we can count on her to continue using him to gather evidence. She usually has him do local legwork."

Aunt Jinny frowned but didn't argue.

Will offered to treat Harriet to fish and chips at Cliffside Chippy before they headed out to Martha's farm.

"Sounds great," Harriet agreed. "Can Benji eat anything soft like mushy peas yet, Aunt Jinny?"

"No, I advise my new mums not to introduce solid foods until baby is six months. Benji is only eight and a half weeks. But he just finished a bottle, so he should be good while you two get something to eat."

Twenty minutes later, Harriet and Will were munching fish and chips, talking to Benji, and enjoying the view from one of the restaurant's outdoor patio tables. Toward the end of their meal, Harriet saw Ronnie Reynolds dash into the shop and emerge a few minutes later with three takeout boxes.

"Did you see that?" she asked Will.

"Yeah, so?"

"Ronnie and Rhys are a two-man team. Why'd they buy three boxes?"

"They're hungry."

Harriet closed her box and tossed her empty soda can in the recycle bin then grabbed Benji's car seat handle. "Come on. We need to follow them."

"What? Why?" Will tossed his nearly empty container into the trash.

Lowering her voice as she hurried off the patio, Harriet said, "Because Ronnie and Rhys had motive, means, and opportunity to take the painting. And the extra box of food has rocketed them to the top of my suspect list."

"How do you figure?" Will relieved Harriet of the baby carrier, allowing her to pick up her pace.

"Mostly because the painting disappeared the same day Rowena did, and Aunt Jinny is adamant that Rowena would never steal anything or abandon her baby. So we were wondering if maybe she witnessed the robbery and hid Benji under the bushes to keep him safe."

"You think they're holding her captive?"

"I think it's worth checking out. As valuable as my grandad's painting might be, it wouldn't bring the kind of money someone would need to set up a new life somewhere under a new identity."

"Which means whoever took it has to stick around and can't afford to let Rowena go, because she could identify them."

"Exactly. They're probably scrambling to figure out a solution." Harriet opened her vehicle's back door so Will could secure the car seat. "I'm afraid it's only a matter of time before they decide it's them or her."

The pest control van pulled onto the road.

"There they go. Get in." Harriet edged onto the street one car behind the van. "If we're lucky, they'll lead us to where they're holding her. Then we can bide our time until they leave for their next job, and rescue her." She tightened her grip on the steering wheel and prayed the pair weren't delivering the woman her last meal.

She gasped as another thought hit her.

"What is it?" Will's voice vibrated with concern.

"They likely stock several different poisons in their company vehicle. What if they're injecting Rowena's meal with it as we speak?"

"Do you really think they'd risk killing her in a way that could be traced back to them so easily?"

Harriet sped up and passed the car between them. "They might be planning to dump her body on a deserted moor, figuring that by the time she's found, the authorities will assume she fell while out for a walk or something. And if Van or DI McCormick has already spoken to them, they'll know they don't have much time to move the painting and get Rowena as far away from them as possible."

"Don't you think you might be jumping to conclusions? This all sounds a bit far-fetched to me."

Harriet gritted her teeth. "Maybe. But there's only one way to find out."

Ahead, the van turned onto a narrow lane.

Harriet slammed her brakes then glanced in the rearview mirror to see if Benji was still okay. Thankfully, the motion of the vehicle had lulled him to sleep. "I remember Polly telling me the ruins of an old castle are around here somewhere. Maybe they stashed her there."

"The ruins are to the east. Doreen Danby's sister Maureen lives here."

"Her sister Elaine is a client at the clinic, but I didn't realize they had another sister. I don't believe I've met Maureen."

"She doesn't get out much. She's not fond of crowds. But her raspberry scones are almost as good as her sister's almond apricot scones."

Harriet waited until the van disappeared into the trees between the road and the house. "What should we do?"

"Go ahead and drive up to the house. It's about time I pay Maureen a visit anyway. A couple of months ago a few of the church's young people cleared away an old tree that had fallen in her yard. I'll ask if she has any other needs we can help with. My dropping in to ask won't seem suspicious, since our little group usually cleans her gutters after the leaves fall. While I'm talking to Maureen, I'll find out why she has Ronnie and Rhys here, and you can have a poke around."

"What about Benji?" She glanced in the rearview mirror again. Benji was still sleeping, and thankfully, so was the fawn, sprawled out in the blanketed cage Polly had supplied them for the trip. "We can't leave him unattended in a vehicle."

"I'll take him with me. Maureen might enjoy seeing a wee one."

Harriet parked behind the van in the shade of a giant tree so she could see inside when they opened the back doors. "You can leave Benji. I'll wait here. Maybe I'll get a chance to look in the van windows if I see you're keeping them busy or if they go inside." She rolled down her window to better hear what was said.

"Brilliant." Will let himself out. "Hey, fellas," he called to Ronnie and Rhys. "What's invaded poor Maureen's place?" Will had his minister's collar on, so he had the advantage of the question seeming innocent enough. And if one of the guys walked around to the back of the van and questioned why Harriet was chauffeuring him, he could tell them about his totaled car and the orphaned fawn.

"Bees in the attic," Ronnie said.

The three men traipsed up to the house and waited at the door for Maureen. After a few minutes with still no sign of her, Harriet heard Will say, "She's probably in her garden. I can wait here in case she comes through if you two want to check there."

The men agreed and each took a side of the house to go around.

The instant they disappeared from view, Harriet slipped out of the Land Rover and opened the rear doors of the van. No Rowena. Not that Harriet had expected to find the woman trussed up inside the vehicle a day after she'd gone missing. She scrutinized the van's floor for any evidence Rowena had been there, such as a scrap of cloth, scuff marks, a feminine scent, or even a scribbled note in the dust or other stealthily dropped clue.

Unfortunately, the van was immaculate, and everything was meticulously stored. The trouble was, Harriet hadn't seen in the back of the truck yesterday to know if that was status quo or an attempt to cover up a crime.

Harriet shut the doors as quietly as she could and crept around to open the driver's door. Two of the takeaway containers were empty and stuffed in a trash bag. The third sat between the two front seats. Harriet glanced toward Benji and then out the front windshield to make sure no one was coming. She pulled the box closer and opened the lid.

Two giant sausages sat inside. Okay, that wasn't what she'd expected. She scrutinized them, but neither appeared tampered with in any way. Maybe Will had been right about the men being extra hungry, or maybe they used sausage to bait traps.

Noticing they had a keyless ignition and had left the fob on the seat, Harriet held her breath and touched the ignition button twice. Then she tapped the screen to find the GPS navigation history for the last day or so. *Interesting.* They had been to two other places yesterday besides the art gallery and their house, and this was their third stop today. They'd visited one of the locations both yesterday and today. She snapped a picture of the screen with her phone then tapped the ignition button again to shut off the display.

The hair on the back of her neck prickled a second before someone behind her cleared his throat. "Can I help you?" Ronnie's gruff voice sounded close to her ear.

CHAPTER EIGHT

At the man's incensed tone, sweat broke out on Harriet's brow. She straightened quickly, scrambling for an excuse as to why she'd been poking around the van. "Uh, yeah, I was wondering—how many miles does she get to the gallon?"

"Excuse me?"

"The van." She motioned to her Land Rover. "I'd like to replace that monster with an automatic. This one seems about the right size to store my vet equipment."

"Oh." His shoulders relaxed, and his voice lost the threatening note. "Mileage isn't too bad. Be better than yours, I'd think. Why are you here? Maureen doesn't have any animals."

"Uh, no." With her back pressed against the van's sun-warmed steel, Harriet edged toward her vehicle. The quiet burbles of a waking baby drifted through her vehicle's open window—a baby she'd prefer Ronnie knew nothing about. "The pastor needed a lift, so I volunteered."

"Ronnie?" shouted his brother. "You coming or what?"

"Yeah, keep your shirt on."

"Sorry for holding you up." Harriet practically dove into the Land Rover at the same time Will climbed in the passenger side.

"Everything okay?" he asked.

Harriet fired up the engine, reversed away from the van, and then executed a tight turn to drive out. "Is Benji okay?" she asked too loudly and immediately worried he'd react to the tension in her voice.

Will leaned over the back of his seat. "Still sleeping."

Harriet's breath whooshed from her lungs in a relieved sigh. She stopped at the end of the driveway and took a moment to fasten her seat belt. "That was close."

"Did you find something incriminating?"

"I'm not sure yet. Do Ronnie and Rhys strike you as the kind of guys who'd have a truck so clean you could eat off the floor?"

"They are in pest control, so they'd know garbage attracts pests."

"Or they scrubbed it clean to hide any evidence that could prove they stashed Rowena in there yesterday." Harriet knew she was starting to sound paranoid. But she'd never seen a van so clean.

"What did they do with the takeaway they bought?"

"Two containers were empty, and the third was full of sausages." She shook her head. "I didn't even realize Cliffside Chippy sold sausages. I don't know what to make of it. And I'm not sure Ronnie bought my story about why I was snooping around."

"Sorry. I didn't see him come back, or I would've whistled or something."

"It's okay." Harriet brought up the photo she'd taken of the van's navigation system and handed her phone to Will. "I did find this."

"What am I looking at?"

"Everywhere that van has been since it left Cobble Hill yesterday." She pointed to the location where it had sat for twelve hours. "I'm assuming that's where they live, which I would hope Van has checked out. So we need to look at the other places they've been." She tapped the location that appeared twice—once immediately following their time at Cobble Hill, and then again that morning. "This one in particular. It could be where they're holding Rowena."

"*If* they're holding Rowena," Will reminded her.

"Yes, if."

Clunks came from the cage in the back of the truck.

"Sounds as if the fawn is getting restless. We better take him to Martha's place before we do anything else," Will said.

Harriet pulled onto the road, hoping it was only her imagination that had made Will sound as if he thought she was leading him on a wild-goose chase.

The Beast backfired, sending the cattle in a nearby field running. They were as jittery as she felt. And the threatening gray clouds overhead didn't help her mood.

A little light to show us the way would really be appreciated here, Lord. Her gaze slanted to her phone screen, and her hopes resurged. Maybe He'd done one better and given her a map to show her the way. *Please don't let my nosing around their van prompt them to take drastic action.*

Harriet's pulse kept racing all the way to the farm. "Do you think we should send the location list to Van?" she asked as she drew up to the house.

"No. I think we should follow up on them before we involve the police." Will got out and lifted the fawn from the cage in the back of the truck as Harriet unbuckled Benji, who was wide awake. "You have a keen sense of observation. Picking up on the three takeaway dinners the Reynolds brothers ordered proved that. But I'm not sure it's enough evidence to convince Van to drive around the country-side retracing Rhys and Ronnie's route."

"Good point. And if they turn out to be our culprits, I'll never forgive myself if we could've stopped them and didn't even try." She grabbed the bag Aunt Jinny had stocked with supplies, hoping Mrs. Banks wouldn't mind warming a bottle for Benji while they were there.

A compact woman carrying a pitchfork and sporting mud-stained overalls over a bright orange shirt came around the side of the barn. Spotting them, she jabbed the pitchfork into the dirt next to the barn and came to meet them.

"Mrs. Banks?" Harriet asked.

"That's right. You the vet?"

"Yes, I'm Harriet Bailey. This is Pastor Will Knight, who found the fawn. We can't thank you enough for agreeing to take it in."

"Call me Martha." The woman had a soft voice that belied her obvious hardworking nature and sported the most glorious long silver hair Harriet had ever seen. She wore it tied up in a ponytail, and Harriet couldn't help but admire her wholehearted embrace of the symbol of her age.

She led them through a crimson-colored door into the long, squat, red-tile-roofed stone barn and motioned to a stall that looked as if it had been prepared for the fawn. "We'll keep him here for a few days until he gets used to the place before letting him out to pasture."

Harriet noticed that Martha didn't have the Yorkshire accent, which made Harriet suspect she had moved to the area from some-where else. But she definitely had a British accent, so she clearly hadn't come from all the way across the pond as Harriet had.

Will settled his precious bundle in the straw. *Cozy* was the description that came to Harriet's mind. Unlike many of the barns she encountered on her farm visits, rife with cobwebs and dimly lit, this barn's windows sat open in their bright-blue frames, allowing fresh air and what sunshine there was to stream in.

The fawn immediately rose and investigated his new home under the watchful eye of a barn cat lazing on a windowsill. Will stayed with the fawn while Harriet showed Benji the rest of Martha's menagerie, housed in the surrounding pasture—five goats of various ages, a miniature horse, and a young fallow deer, besides the ducks populating the pond and the hens enjoying the shade under a sweeping shrub row of rhododendrons.

"Australorp?" Harriet asked, admiring the black-feathered hen that ventured out to see if she had a treat. Its feathers glistened a gorgeous shade of emerald in the sunlight.

"That's right. Australorps are my favorite. Besides being easy to keep and cold-hardy, which we need up here in the winter, their docile nature makes them great around children. We get a lot of young families stopping by to see the animals."

"That's marvelous."

When Will joined them, Martha invited them to the house to heat Benji's bottle.

Will chuckled at the sight of a giant potbellied pig lounging on a patio swing on the shaded front porch. "You don't see that every day."

Martha laughed. "That's Arnold. They say pigs are highly intelligent, but I'm afraid Arnold hasn't figured out that he's not human."

"I'd say he knows exactly what he's doing." Harriet scratched the friendly pig behind the ears, enjoying his satisfied snorts. "Living the good life, aren't you, boy?"

"That's for sure," Martha agreed. "Come on in."

Harriet kept her reason for babysitting deliberately vague, but Martha apparently recognized the redheaded infant. "It must be hard for Rowena," she mused. "Her husband's work is so unpredictable."

Harriet sat at the kitchen table, holding Benji. "What does he do?" she asked. The fact the man still hadn't responded to Aunt Jinny's messages more than twenty-four hours after his wife was last seen was bizarre to say the least.

"I'm not sure exactly." Martha bustled about the kitchen, filling the kettle with water and pulling cups and saucers from the cupboard. "Would you like tea?"

"That would be lovely," Harriet said, and Will agreed.

"Clive is a volunteer with the RNLI, like my eldest son, George," Martha continued. "They're both with the lifeboat crew. I met Rowena at one of their fundraisers."

"My assistant told me about the RNLI and all that the volunteers do," Harriet said. "It's fabulous. I think the coast guard handles those situations in the States. Maybe with the help of police boats. I lived in Connecticut but never thought enough about it to find out who handles what."

"Do the volunteers meet regularly to train?" Will asked.

"Yes. Besides White Church Bay's lifeboat crew, there's a shore crew and a team of lifeguards."

"I imagine they get to know one another well."

"Yes," Martha said. "They're good folk." She reached for Benji. "Here, let me give Benji his bottle while you enjoy your tea. It's been a long time since I've had a little one around to dote on."

Since Benji didn't seem to object, Harriet relinquished the task in favor of stockpiling caffeine to combat the mind fog that had started to set in. "You mentioned Clive's work is unpredictable, but you have no idea what he does for a living?"

"No. Have you asked Rowena?"

Heat flooded Harriet's cheeks. That was exactly the kind of question she'd hoped to avoid. "I can't reach her at the moment, so I was hoping I might contact her husband."

"I see. I'm afraid I can't help with that. I only know that when the call goes out for volunteers, Clive is a no-show about half the time. In the old days, when the crew was needed, a signal went off, and anyone who could make it rushed to the lifeboat station. These days, volunteers are on call on specific days, and we use cell phones to notify them of an emergency. But Clive isn't part of the on-call schedule. I suppose he shows up whenever he's able."

"That's interesting."

"My son might know how you can reach him and perhaps even where he works. Geoff is mending the gate in the second pasture today. I can walk you over after you finish your tea."

Fifteen minutes later, with Benji nestled next to Will's chest in the baby carrier, they stood in the pasture admiring the cutest sheep Harriet had ever seen. "Are these Valais Blacknose sheep?"

"They are, though they're not purebred."

Harriet smiled at the pair of *gimmers*—year-old ewes. With their black heads and ears and black nose, knees, and feet, they resembled adorable stuffed animals rather than living animals. "These originated in Switzerland," she explained to Will.

"They're cute. From a distance, I didn't realize they weren't the usual Scottish Blackface you see throughout the moors."

"Yes, we have some of those around here too," Martha said. "They're probably enjoying the shade under the trees somewhere."

As they walked, Harriet reflected on how she never tired of the sight of pastures enclosed by stone walls and interspersed with woodlands as far as the eye could see across the moors. Delicate blooms of purple betony dotted the shrub row, attracting a steady hum of bees and colorful butterflies. She could just make out the red rooftops of the buildings in White Church Bay and the stormy North Sea. A cool breeze whispered across the fields with a top note of fresh-mown grass and blooming hydrangeas in the garden surrounding Martha's house.

When they reached a man working on a pasture gate, Martha introduced Harriet and Will to him and then asked if he knew where Clive worked.

Geoff set the gate he'd been mending back on its hinges, whipped off his hat, and swiped the sweat from his brow with his shirt sleeve. "He works with the coast guard. Former navy man, I believe."

"Do you know where he's stationed?" Will asked.

"Whitby, I imagine, living around here. We used to have an old coast guard station right in White Church Bay, you know," he said to Harriet.

"Yes, I went through the museum as a kid."

"Being on the coast, our little town was a right haunt for smugglers back in the day. All those fisherman's cottages are connected by underground passages the smugglers used. They called their work 'free trade' because it was the only way to get luxury goods to the common people without paying exorbitant import taxes."

Will nodded. "I read somewhere that they could unload tobacco, tea, silk, and more from boats and move them to the top of the hill and onto the moors without them ever seeing the light of day."

Geoff put his hat back on. "Truth be told, we're certain a few of our lifeboat rescues were for would-be smugglers who were no match for the North Sea. After one rescue not too long ago, old paintings floated to shore with the next tide."

"Paintings?" Harriet's interest piqued.

She exchanged a glance with Will. Could her grandfather's painting already be halfway across the North Sea—and Rowena with it? An uncomfortable thought pricked her at the prospect. If Rowena's husband was involved in the painting's theft and her disappearance, being in the coast guard would give him the knowledge to evade capture.

"Okay, well, thank you for your help." Will glanced at his watch. "We should be off."

"One more thing," Geoff called after them as they started back to the truck. "I heard you have yourself a mysterious outbreak at Goose Beck Farm."

Harriet grimaced. She'd feared the town's grapevine wouldn't take long to spread the word.

"Did you know Staveley's neighbor has been angling for years to buy him out?"

Harriet cocked her head, curious about the hint of implication in his voice. "No, I didn't."

"Aye. If Staveley loses his fold, I suspect he'd be more inclined to sell."

"Are you implying that Gilbert Vail would deliberately poison his neighbor's cows to further his own ends?" Will asked.

"I didn't say that."

"But it's what you're thinking."

Geoff shrugged. "Cattle are curious. They can get themselves into trouble all on their own. I've seen 'em lick old tractor batteries left lying around and make themselves sick. When I was a teen, we had a goat lap up antifreeze. Remember that, Mum?"

Martha nodded soberly.

Harriet sighed. Sadly, she'd seen too many accidental poisonings in her practice, even from things as seemingly benign as a dog eating grapes or onions. And when she'd first seen Mr. Staveley's calf, she'd suspected poison. But with several more cows exhibiting similar symptoms and no obvious source of poison, the best she could hope for was that the quarantine would keep more animals from succumbing before the blood tests told them what poison they needed to locate.

"Only I didn't know what the fool goat had done," Geoff continued. "I thought it was comical to see her acting drunk and didn't realize what she got into until Mum and Dad got home the next morning. And by then it was too late to save her."

Harriet cringed, her fear mounting that she would be too late. Too late to save Grandad's painting from the hands of a greedy collector and too late to save Mr. Staveley's cattle.

And worst of all, too late to save Benji's mother.

CHAPTER NINE

Harriet typed the destinations from the Reynolds brothers' GPS history into the map app on her phone while Will strapped Benji into his car seat in the back. "I want to prioritize the location they hit twice. But there's another stop between here and there that we might as well visit first."

"Sounds good." Will belted himself into the front seat. "Should I navigate?"

Harriet handed him her phone. "Thanks. Hopefully the system won't drop when we dip into the valleys. But at least I know this place. It's near Goose Beck Farm. Although I can't say I noticed their van anywhere about when I was in the area." Harriet set off. By the time she saved enough to replace her grandad's old vehicle with one that included a navigation system, she'd probably know all the White Church Bay roads backward and forward.

"Turn left at the next bend," Will instructed. "The location should be less than a mile down the road on the right."

Harriet frowned. "There aren't any buildings on this stretch of road. Do you think they had an accomplice meet them?"

"Stop here," Will said.

Harriet hit the brakes.

Will jumped out of the vehicle and traipsed back along the road, scouring the ditch.

Harriet undid her seat belt, but by the time she climbed out and opened the rear door to get Benji out, Will was already returning.

"You can see by the flattened grass that a large vehicle pulled to the side of the road. Then there's a path to the steps built into the stone wall. It's not well-defined, mind you, and there's no trail on the other side of the wall."

"What do you think they were doing?"

"There's a flattened rectangle of grass on the other side of the wall. I suspect they released whatever critters they'd captured."

"My gray squirrels?"

"Probably not. It's illegal to relocate gray squirrels in the UK, because they're an invasive species. They might have had an animal on board from the place they went before coming here."

"The place by Goose Beck Farm."

"Yeah."

"One way to find out." Harriet climbed back into the car. She'd been expecting, or at least hoping, to find an abandoned barn or cottage where they'd stashed Rowena and the painting after leaving Cobble Hill, not the location of another pest control job.

She sped toward the Staveley farm, well-acquainted with the dips and curves in the road. She braced herself for a steep descent and subsequent incline then spotted the lone building sitting in a field not far from the Staveleys'. "Are we getting close?"

"Not yet."

She passed the decrepit barn and neared Goose Beck Farm. "Now?"

"Nope. It's still farther."

Spotting the neighboring farm on the horizon, she said, "Getting close now?"

"Yes. It looks as if they stopped at the Vail farm."

Harriet slowed as she neared the driveway.

"Wait, I'm wrong. We're not quite there," Will said.

"There's nothing but pastureland farther on." Or maybe another abandoned barn? Her pulse spiked.

"There." Will pointed to a weed-infested lane.

"Can you see where it goes?"

"No, but I know where it goes—a small, one-story cottage. Gilbert Vail's mother-in-law lives here."

Harriet's heart sank. "So no chance they're keeping Rowena or my grandfather's painting here." Not that she wanted that, but she was ready for some answers.

"Let's find out." Will hopped out of the truck before Harriet had the engine off.

A tiny woman in a bright red headscarf stepped off the porch, gripping the head of a polo mallet in her gnarled fingers and using the shaft as a walking stick. "Is that you, Pastor?" she called. She squinted suspiciously in Harriet's direction.

"Hello, Eva May. My car's in the shop, and the new vet has been kind enough to give me a ride." He introduced Harriet to the woman.

Hovering near her open truck door and wondering if she should get Benji out, Harriet waved. "Nice to meet you."

Will closed the distance between him and Eva May. "I understand the Reynolds brothers have been out here. Are you having an issue with pests?"

Eva May nodded. "Had a swarm of bees trying to make a new home in the attic."

"Maureen had the same problem."

"The boys came last week and gathered most of them by simply tipping them into a cardboard box from the swarm under the overhang"—she motioned the tip of her makeshift cane toward the eaves on her cottage—"then relocated them after dark. But quite a few had already managed to get into the house, so they had to come back and take care of those. Did that yesterday afternoon."

Will nodded. "Did they come out this way again earlier today?"

"Aye. When they were here yesterday, I asked if they could catch whatever has been eating my guinea fowl, and they set up a few traps. They came by this morning and found a stoat in one of them, so they took it away."

If the woman thought it was strange for Will to be so curious about the brothers' comings and goings to the point of driving all the way out here to ask about them, she didn't say so. Harriet studied the small yard. There were no outbuildings besides the henhouse. No place to stash a painting or a would-be witness.

Benji started to fuss. "I think he wants to get moving," Harriet called to Will, who thanked Eva May and got back into the truck.

"It's a dead end, I'm afraid," he said.

Expelling a heavy sigh, Harriet reversed out of the lane. "And it seems unlikely they would've risked leaving Rowena in the van while visiting a client. Maybe one dropped off the other with Rowena somewhere along the route."

Will shook his head. "She said they were both there each time."

"Well, I guess the positive side to this is we can cross the Reynolds brothers off our suspect list." Harriet slowed as she drove past the Vail farm, her thoughts returning to what Geoff had suggested about Gilbert Vail poisoning the Staveleys' cows. "Are you in a hurry to get back to town?"

"Not particularly."

"Good. Because I'd like to take a walk." She glanced in her rearview mirror. "Would you like that, Benji?"

The baby didn't protest, which she took as a good sign.

Will must have detected the hope in her voice, because he tipped his head curiously. "Did you have a particular place in mind?"

"Yes, the moorlands where the Staveley cows graze. Like Geoff Banks said, cows are curious beasts. They'll lick whatever they come across the same way Benji explores his world by putting things in his mouth. Maybe we can find what's poisoned them."

"Didn't Mr. Staveley inspect the field after he found his cows sick?"

"I'm sure he did. But maybe someone dumped something on the side of the road that's toxic to cows and he missed it."

"Gilbert Vail isn't that kind of bloke," Will said defensively. "Not to mention he wouldn't put his own cattle at risk by dumping something where they could get to it."

"I didn't say it was his doing." Harriet wondered whether Will had such confidence in everyone in his flock, or if something about Gilbert made him so sure of the man's ethics. "There's a public pathway through the pasture. It could have been anyone."

"Okay, I'm game to have a look. A walk would be nice."

Harriet parked down the road from Goose Beck Farm, preferring that Mr. Staveley didn't know what she was up to. He might take offense that she hadn't trusted him to adequately scout the field.

They walked along the public path then veered away from it, since no one was likely to litter anything more than a candy wrapper or soda can where a rambler would trip over it.

She kept a wary eye on the cattle grazing in the valley below that Gilbert Vail had apparently opted to leave in the common field. They were mostly tawny-colored Highlands with their young calves, along with several black-and-white Belted Galloways. Although cows were typically gentle creatures, and Highlands seemed especially friendly, they were all highly protective of their calves. She'd heard stories about them stampeding in the presence of ramblers, causing serious injury and even the odd death. She didn't want to take any chances with Benji in their care.

After forty-five minutes of combing meadows and bushes, Benji began to fuss.

"We'd better call it a day." Harriet bounced the boy in the carrier to no avail. "I left his bottle back in the truck."

Will took him from her. "Up for a jog?"

"Let's make it a fast walk."

As they crested a hill, several children dashed across the dale in front of them. "I think those are Mr. Staveley's grandchildren. We should ask them to be on the lookout for potentially dangerous litter," Will suggested.

"Good idea." Harriet waved to get their attention and motioned them over.

They shuffled their feet, clearly reluctant to talk to her.

Will chuckled. "Looks as if they think they're in trouble."

"They might be if their grandad discovers they're out here. After sending the boys to bring in the rest of his cows this morning, he told Abby she wasn't to go in the field."

"What have you kids been up to?" Will asked as they neared.

"Nothing," the oldest boy answered for all of them. He shushed Abby when she started to speak.

Harriet explained what they were searching for and asked if she could enlist their help.

They all seemed to grow a couple of inches at the request and eagerly agreed to let her know if they found anything on their way back to their grandfather's farm. "There's an old barn in the next dale," Abby said. "But Grandad said we shouldn't play there. Because it's dangerous."

"Oh?" Harriet squinted in the direction Abby indicated and was able to make out the corner of the barn that she'd spotted on her first visit to Goose Beck Farm. "Can the cows get inside it?"

"No," the older boy said. "The timbers are rotted. That's why Grandad told us not to play there."

"I see." Harriet nevertheless glanced that way once more, wondering if the sick cows might have found a way in despite what the farmer's grandson believed.

A couple of ramblers crested the hill in front of the barn, and the sight of them triggered something in Harriet's memory. Where had she seen them before?

At Benji's whimper, Will reminded her they'd better keep moving.

Harriet speed-walked alongside him, but her gaze kept drifting to the couple in the distance. Although they appeared older, they moved at a good clip. They both carried pairs of walking sticks, one in each hand. The man turned, and Harriet finally placed them. "It's the couple with the oversize rucksacks."

"Pardon?" Will asked over Benji's protests.

Harriet squinted at the pair. "I think they might be the same couple. It took me a couple of minutes to remember them."

Will frowned in the direction she pointed. "Remember them from where?"

"The art gallery. They were there the day we discovered the painting was stolen. They could have easily walked out with it hidden in one of those packs."

The couple disappeared down the hill.

Harriet picked up her pace. "They're getting away." She headed toward the Land Rover, which was closer than the couple. "We can intercept them when they reach the road farther on."

Will jogged alongside her, sounding barely winded from the exertion, despite carrying the baby. "How can you be sure it's the same couple?"

"Their rucksacks. Most ramblers carry small ones, big enough to hold a drink and snacks, perhaps a raincoat."

"I don't know. The people doing the DofE have to camp overnight, so they carry big ones."

"D of E?"

"The Duke of Edinburgh Award. It's a program that awards young people for completing a series of self-improvement exercises, like volunteering, skills development, expeditions, and physical activities. It's for participants age fourteen to twenty-four."

"This couple is older than that," Harriet said.

"Okay." Will held his hand out. "Give me the keys. I'll run ahead and get Benji buckled in."

Harriet dug them out of her pocket and passed them to him.

His strides lengthened, and she fell behind.

By the time she reached the truck, Benji was buckled in and temporarily mollified by the pacifier they'd left in his car seat. Will tossed her the keys, and she jumped into the driver's side. She slammed the gas pedal, and soon they crested a steep incline. "Can you see them?"

"A silver car disappeared over the next hill." Will twisted in his seat and peered every which way. "That had to be them. They must've been parked nearby. I don't see anyone else out here, and no cars passed us after I got to the truck."

"Keep your eyes peeled." Harriet sped toward the valley below, slowing as they neared the overgrown trackway leading to the dilapidated old barn.

"A vehicle has definitely been here recently." Will pointed to the parallel lines of flattened weeds on the side of the road.

"Let's catch them."

CHAPTER TEN

Harriet slowed as she entered the upper end of White Church Bay. She scanned driveways, sidewalks, and parking lots, but it was no use. "We lost them."

"Report your suspicions to Van," Will said from the passenger seat. "Or ask Mrs. Winslow about the couple. I'm sure she'd remember anyone coming into the gallery with walking sticks and rucksacks. And she'd be able to tell you if they're local or not."

"Good idea."

"If they aren't from around here, Van can check with the locals to see if anyone knows where they're staying. "

"You're right." The rearview mirror showed Benji's arm flailing. The vehicle's motion had lulled him back to sleep earlier, but unfortunately the crawl she'd slowed to no longer seemed to be doing the trick. "I'd better drop you home and get Benji to Aunt Jinny's for his next feeding." She'd been silly to race across the countryside after the silver car that might not have even belonged to the couple. She parked in front of the rectory. "For all I know, Mrs. Winslow already mentioned the pair to the police. After all, Van did question her."

"True, but there's no harm in them hearing about the couple again." Will climbed out of the truck. "Although, if I'd nicked your painting, I wouldn't hang around waiting to be caught."

"I get that, but I was thinking about what Geoff Banks said about smugglers. This couple could be professional art thieves who stationed themselves here to fill an unscrupulous collector's shopping list. After all, no one would ever suspect them." Her face heated at how wild her idea must sound. But finding a baby alone in the bushes like Moses in the bulrushes was pretty unbelievable too.

"I think Van might have mentioned if there'd been other art stolen in the area," Will pointed out.

She twisted her hands on the steering wheel, hating how helpless she felt. "I'll ask him."

"Okay. Keep me posted on what you learn. And thanks for helping with the fawn." Will shut the truck door with a wave.

Benji startled at the sound.

"Don't you fret, bud. I'm taking you back to Aunt Jinny now. Then I'll see if our nice detective constable can find Mr. and Mrs. Rucksack and your mummy." Harriet pictured how the pair had arrived at the gallery from the pasture. They looked as if they'd been hiking for a while, which meant they'd likely left their car in town. So if Rowena had spotted them taking the painting, how would they have convinced her to leave with them? Was one of those smuggling tunnels close enough to Cobble Hill that they could have muscled her out of sight without anyone noticing?

Surely Grandad would've mentioned a tunnel entrance if he'd known about it. Then again, maybe not. He would have known she'd be too inquisitive to resist exploring it.

Mrs. Winslow was locking the front door of the gallery as Harriet drove in.

Harriet drew up alongside her and asked if she'd mind waiting a few minutes. She delivered Benji back to Aunt Jinny's care with a kiss on top of his head then found Mrs. Winslow waiting on a bench in the garden.

When Harriet described the couple, Mrs. Winslow's face lit with recognition. "I remember them. They're from south of London on a fortnight's vacation in town to take in the sights."

"Did they mention where they were staying?"

Mrs. Winslow's gaze shifted skyward as if she was searching her memory. "Not that I recall."

"Did you mention the couple to Van when he questioned you about the theft?"

Her eyes widened. "You can't think that lovely couple would take your painting."

"I don't know what to think about any of this," Harriet said glumly.

"Van collected copies of yesterday's gallery receipts. But I think that couple paid cash, so he wouldn't have gotten their information from me." Mrs. Winslow's brow furrowed. "And I don't think I mentioned them to him. Perhaps I should consider requiring names and contact information for cash receipts. I didn't think of it before now because I handwrite the cash receipts, and I was going for efficiency. But now I'm coming up with all kinds of uses for more information. I may start doing that."

"That sounds like a good idea," Harriet told her. "In the meantime, I'll speak to Van about the couple."

Mrs. Winslow consulted her watch. "I expect you'll find him at the cricket pitch by now. He's helping to coach a group of youngsters this summer."

"Thanks." Harriet said goodbye, and they parted.

A yip alerted Harriet that Polly had left Maxwell in the side garden before heading home. Harriet trotted around the house and received a joyous welcome from the little dachshund. "Hey, Maxwell. I'm afraid I'm heading out again, but I'll give you your supper before I go. You want to come in?"

The dog wheeled himself over to a little bench then rose and rested his front legs and chest on it. He almost seemed to sigh as he laid his muzzle on his front paws.

"I guess that's a no. You sure know how to make a girl feel guilty, don't you?" She scratched his head. "You're a good boy. I shouldn't be gone long." Fifteen minutes later, after freshening up and giving Maxwell his supper, Harriet drove to the cricket pitch.

Scanning the field as she climbed out of the car, she couldn't spot Van. Harriet tapped the shoulder of one of the moms on the sidelines. "Excuse me. Do you know if Van Worthington will be here tonight?"

"He was earlier, but he got called to a motor accident."

"Oh dear. Okay, thank you." Heading back to her car, Harriet noticed a vehicle leaving the RV camp nearby, often called a caravan park. Mr. and Mrs. Rucksack seemed like the outdoorsy type who might opt to vacation in a caravan park rather than an inn or B&B. And since she'd been to the White Church Bay Caravan Park a few weeks ago to care for the owner's horse, her arrival shouldn't raise any suspicions. She'd meant to stop in again sometime anyway to check up on the horse.

Arlene Metcalfe, the fiftysomething co-owner of the place, came out of the stable as Harriet drove in. A wide smile replaced the initial surprise on her round face, and she hurried over to the Land Rover. "Have you come to check on Sparkle?"

Harriet jumped out of her truck. "Yes, how's he doing?"

"Grand, thanks to you. He's got his spark back, if you'll excuse the joke."

"Terrific. Is it all right if I check him myself? No charge, of course." Harriet tugged on the pair of wellies, or Wellington boots, she kept behind the driver's seat.

"Oh, brilliant. Thank you."

Many farmers put off calling Harriet because making a living at farming was hard enough without adding unexpected vet bills to the mix. Some had gotten creative about supplementing their farming income. The Metcalfes had turned a few acres of their land into a caravan park.

Sparkle trotted to the corral fence at Arlene's call.

Harriet stroked the horse's neck as she examined him. "You're right. He seems to be doing great."

"He is. I'm glad I called you."

Making no move to suggest she was in a hurry to leave, Harriet shifted to scan the caravan park. "Looks as if this is a popular place."

"This time of year it is. People come to walk the moors or cliffs or hunt for fossils on the beach."

"We had a pair of ramblers visit my grandfather's gallery this week. Each of them carried two walking sticks and a large rucksack. Are they staying here?" She asked the last part in a casual tone, hoping it sounded like idle curiosity.

"No, but I think I know who you mean. We had a couple of that description stop in at the beginning of the week, hoping to snag the small efficiency cabin we rent out, but it was already booked. I suggested they try the White Hart. They'd already been to the Crow's Nest, so I was able to give them directions from there to the inn. I can't say if they'll be at the White Hart, but I imagine someone at the Crow's Nest would be able to help."

Harriet recalled the first time her grandad took her to the White Hart Inn, which also featured a good restaurant. The place managed to give off both grand and cozy vibes simultaneously. The Crow's Nest, on the other hand, had a great pub atmosphere, with excellent food and frequent events so that the community had an excuse to get together.

"I'm glad to hear they must've found a place to stay in the area," Arlene added.

"Yes, they seemed like a nice couple."

"And fascinating to chat with. Before the man retired, he was a fellow at Oxford University in the art history program. I remember that detail because my nephew was considering that program."

"Art history? That is interesting." And by interesting, she meant suspicious.

The arrival of a truck towing a caravan captured Arlene's attention, giving Harriet the perfect excuse to cut the conversation short, get back in the Land Rover, and head for the Crow's Nest, since Arlene said they'd been there. It was in the old section of town, which was better to navigate on foot because of the tight, twisting passageways.

Harriet parked at the top of the hill and exited her vehicle. The public footpath running through the farm connected to the coast-to-coast path along the cliff, and it was her preferred route into the older part of town this time of year.

She nodded and smiled at familiar faces and tourists alike as she began her descent down the steep hill. When she reached Cliffside Chippy, Polly waved from the queue outside and called, "Hey, want to join me for supper?"

"Actually, I ate there for lunch. I'm heading to the Crow's Nest."

Polly slipped out of line and joined Harriet. "I like the sound of that." She lowered her voice. "Best pub food in town. But don't tell the tourists, or the locals will never get a table."

Harriet chuckled. "I'd love to have you come with me. To tell you the truth, I wasn't sure I'd be able to find it by myself. It's off one of these side lanes, right?"

"The next one on the left." Polly edged ahead and started up a short flight of stone steps to a cobbled lane, no more than a footpath that meandered between rows of cottages and soon curved and forked into three more paths.

Harriet had gotten lost more than once chasing childhood friends through the twisting maze during summertime visits. One cottage ran into the next in long lines, but while they seemed to share the same red-tiled roof, one might have a red brick face, the next whitewashed, and the next gray sandstone blocks. They even had different-colored doors and windows, and some had wooden benches in front of them, despite there being scarcely more than a couple of feet between the wall of the house and the path or laneway.

Harriet hadn't been in this section of town since her move. In some places, walls of hedges or ivy flanked one side of the path, providing a dense cover if someone had criminal intent. Not that she'd ever heard of people having trouble with break-ins. Those rarely happened in White Church Bay.

Thankfully, Polly knew every nook and cranny—and quite possibly the rumored smuggling tunnels and secret hiding places beneath their feet.

Harriet caught up to her and lowered her voice. "Have you seen the tunnels the smugglers used to use?"

"Some of them." She grinned. "When I was little, a friend of mine lived in a cottage the next lane over that had a secret hiding place. Most of the cottages do. The tunnel runs under the Crow's Nest. The barkeep uses it as a wine cellar."

"Have you seen it?" Harriet glanced in the direction of Cobble Hill. Could there really be more than a mile of still passable subterranean tunnels between here and there?

"Unfortunately, I haven't. I sure would like to though." Polly raised an eyebrow at her. "Why are you asking?"

Harriet told Polly about the elderly couple she hoped to find at the pub and her theory that they might have stolen the painting and forced Rowena, the witness to their crime, into the tunnels where they wouldn't be seen.

Polly shook her head. "If you could get clear through, someone would have made it into a tourist trap by now."

"Not necessarily, because wouldn't each portion belong to the cottage sitting above it?"

"I don't know. But trust me, if there was a tunnel to be found—beyond the odd bits of them here and there that a few places boast about to draw in customers—my brothers would've found it. Every kid in White Church Bay would."

"You're right. I imagine the county bricked off any entrances accessible to the public because of safety concerns. But the couple could have slipped the painting into one of their rucksacks and hiked out right under everyone's noses with no one the wiser." But where did that leave Rowena?

"Here we are," Polly declared, sweeping her hand toward a door in the wall painted a bright royal blue instead of the deep burgundy Harriet remembered from her teen years.

Inside, the air smelled of ale and fried food. A jovial mood pervaded the U-shaped room with its flagstone floor. Yellow-hued lamplight added to the warm feel of the place. The distressed wood counter was polished to a shiny gleam, and the mirrored wall behind it gave an added sparkle to the glasses and bottles lining the wall. A plaque dated the pub to 1636. Exposed massive wooden beams supported the whitewashed ceiling. Round wooden tables dotted the center of the room, while long narrow tables with settles sat along the walls not occupied by dartboards.

Harriet scanned the faces of the people seated around the tables but didn't spot the couple. "Will you order me a steak and kidney pie and a ginger ale when the server comes? I want to ask at the counter about the couple."

"Will do," Polly said, still poring over her menu.

Harriet made her way to the bar and asked the barkeep about the two hikers. "They're a retired art history professor and his wife."

"You don't know their names?"

"No, sorry." When the man's expression closed off as if he was rethinking the wisdom of divulging the names of his guests to a perfect stranger, Harriet added, "They stopped by my grandfather's art gallery a couple of days ago, and I was hoping to speak to them again."

The man's face lit up. "You're Doc Bailey's granddaughter?"

"That's right."

"I knew Doc. He saved one of my customers right here at the bar from choking on a peanut. He was right quick about it too. Did it before any of us realized what was happening."

Harriet smiled, remembering when Mom passed along that particular tale.

"So, you want to talk to this fellow about art then?"

"Yes." Namely, what he'd done with her grandad's painting and perhaps Rowena. "The man is gray-haired, wiry build, not very tall, maybe five-eight." Harriet couldn't recall any details about his wife, so she added, "They like walking and usually carry big rucksacks and walking sticks. They're maybe in their sixties."

The barkeep stroked his thin mustache with his knuckle, frowning as he seemingly searched his memory. "I can't say I remember seeing a couple with that description."

Harriet deflated. "You're sure?"

"Positive. Sorry I couldn't be of more help."

Harriet took a business card from her purse and handed it to the man. "If they do happen to come in, could you give me a call? I'd really like to chat with them before they leave town."

He glanced at the card then opened his cash register and placed it inside. "Will do."

By the time Harriet thanked him and returned to the table, her ginger ale was waiting for her. She took an icy swig, relishing the cool sweetness. Out on the moors earlier, the temperature had been quite comfortable, but this place, tucked in the maze of back streets, didn't enjoy the breezes off the North Sea. Like most places in the UK, it also didn't have air-conditioning.

"No joy?" Polly asked.

Harriet shook her head. "And short of calling on every B&B, cottage rental, and hotel in town, I don't know where else to try."

"So you've crossed the Reynolds brothers off your suspect list?'

Harriet filled Polly in on how she and Will had followed the brothers from Cliffside Chippy and then retraced their movements using their van's GPS history. "While they *could* have had the painting stashed in their van all that time, it doesn't seem likely they'd trek around the countryside with Rowena after kidnapping her. Though the back of their van was suspiciously clean."

Polly laughed. "I would have found it suspicious in your shoes. But I went to school with Ronnie, and he was a total neat freak. I think Rhys was actually diagnosed with OCD."

Okay. Obsessive-compulsive tendencies would explain the pristine state of their van.

Polly's eyes narrowed at something behind Harriet.

"What is it?" Harriet started to glance over her shoulder, but Polly grabbed her arm to stop her.

"Don't look." Polly lowered her voice. "The two blokes sitting by the window across from the bar are wearing dark sunglasses. They haven't looked away from us since you started talking to the barkeep."

Harriet rolled her eyes at Polly's wild imagination. "You're the hunk magnet, remember? And how can you tell they're watching us if they're wearing sunglasses?"

Polly leaned across the table, her voice dipping even lower. "They keep turning their faces this way. And I don't think they're staring because they think we're cute."

CHAPTER ELEVEN

As Harriet and Polly waited for their meal to be served, trying to ignore the starers by the window, Harriet launched a search on her phone for former lecturers in art history at Oxford. "If we're lucky, maybe I can hit on a name for our guy to give Van more to go on."

Polly took a drink of her soda. "Have you heard whether the forensics expert he brought in from York found anything?"

"What expert? I didn't get back to Cobble Hill until almost five. Mrs. Winslow told me Van had been there to collect receipts but didn't mention a forensics expert."

"I'm not sure he went inside the gallery, so she might not have seen him. As near as I could tell, they were going over footprints and tire tracks. But I don't see what good that'll do them."

Harriet straightened in her chair. "Were they tracking footprints? Maybe the police know about an entrance to the smuggling tunnels that we don't."

"They did go out behind the barns. That's when I spotted the pair of them because Maxwell started barking his head off. But the forensics guy didn't seem happy about Van chatting with me and hurried him off."

Harriet suspected that was because Van's conversation with Polly likely had little to do with their investigation.

Polly sucked in a sharp breath, as if suddenly remembering something. "Did you ask the barkeep if we could see the tunnel?"

"No, but after hearing this bit of news, I'd like to."

Polly grinned. "I'll ask." She added some gloss to her lips, tugged off the elastic holding back her dark hair, and fluffed it about her shoulders.

Harriet leaned forward and whispered, "You do know the barkeep is old enough to be your father, don't you?"

"Not the one that just joined him." Polly tossed Harriet a wink then made her way toward a dark-haired, brown-eyed, twenty-something polishing glasses.

Harriet cast a glance at the table where the men in the sunglasses sat, but they were gone. *Good.* She hadn't relished the idea of winding through the maze of alleyways trying to give them the slip if they decided to get chummy.

Polly rushed back to their table and tugged on Harriet's arm. "We're in."

"Now?" Harriet surged to her feet, not about to complain. Passing the waitress carrying a plate of steak and kidney pie and another of the appetizer sampler, she asked, "Are those for us?"

"Yes."

"Could you keep them warm for a few minutes, please? We shouldn't be long." Harriet didn't dare risk asking Polly's new friend if they could delay the tour until after they ate. By then the pub could be brimming with customers, making it impossible for him to break away.

As they followed the guy down a set of dank, ancient stone steps, Polly shot an excited grin back at Harriet. "Isn't this cool?"

And it was—literally. Cool, damp air engulfed them as they dropped lower into the tunnel.

At the bottom of the stairs, their would-be tour guide veered right and shoved aside a large wooden wardrobe, giving Harriet the sudden sense that they were about to step into another world. He then pulled his phone from his pocket and switched on his flashlight. Polly did the same, so Harriet followed suit.

"This way leads down to the sea," the barkeep explained.

Harriet wasn't sure how far they walked hunched over, trying to avoid contact with the walls and any creatures that might be crawling on them. She shuddered at the thought and aimed her light at the ground to watch for rats and then at the ceiling for bats. This no longer felt like such a good idea. "I'm actually more interested in the tunnel leading to the moors."

The barkeep stopped. "That entrance was bricked off. Do you want to go farther this way? In another ten yards, there are steps down to the stream that flows under the town. I figure that's what they followed out to sea."

"No thanks. We should go eat our meal before it's cold." Since she'd brought up the rear, a dejected Harriet led the way back to the Crow's Nest's cellar, her hope of finding Rowena dimming fast.

"Thanks so much for showing us the tunnel," Polly said to the barkeep. "Do you know if any of the other cottages or pubs have an accessible tunnel that leads up the hill?"

"Not likely," he replied. "We'd get people sneaking from the cottages into our cellars and nicking our stock."

"Good point."

Once back upstairs, Harriet and Polly said little as they ate.

Setting down her knife and fork, Polly glanced toward the rear of the pub. "Fancy a game of darts?"

"No, I should head home. I left Maxwell outside and promised I wouldn't be long." Pulling out her credit card, she chewed on her bottom lip. "I also promised Benji we'd find his parents, and I haven't."

"Benji's abandonment isn't your fault. For all we know, Rowena really could be our thief and took off with an accomplice."

"If we could get in touch with her husband so Benji at least has one parent, that'd be something," Harriet said. "Geoff Banks has worked with Clive in the RNLI and said he works for the coast guard. If he's been stationed overseas, you'd think the police would've been able to reach him through his CO."

Polly shook her head. "Our coast guard isn't military or law enforcement, so I don't know that they would be stationed overseas or that he would have a CO. Geoff could have been thinking that Clive volunteers with the rescue service of His Majesty's Coastguard. They do stuff like search and rescue, help people in trouble on the water, and plenty of other things."

"I don't know. Maybe Geoff has it wrong, because if Clive travels for work a lot, how would he find the time to volunteer for both organizations? I imagine they both have intensive training, right?"

"I dated someone in the coast guard for a couple of months. We could see if he knows Clive," Polly said as she gathered her purse. "If we hurry, we can still catch him at the cricket pitch. He and his mates play every Saturday night."

Several phones around the room rang simultaneously, and a moment later, three guys and a woman hurried out of the pub.

"What's going on?" Harriet asked the waitress who was processing her payment.

"Must be an emergency on the water. A lot of volunteers with the lifeboat crew are regulars here. We often host fundraisers for them—quiz nights and raffles and such."

"Let's get to the lifeboat station," Harriet said to Polly.

They hurried out the door. "If Clive's not responding to Jinny's call about his own son, do you really think he'll respond to the emergency call of a perfect stranger?" Polly asked.

"Only one way to find out."

By the time they reached the lifeboat station, a couple dozen men and women were gathered near the lifeboat. Seagulls bobbed in the water around it.

"Do you see Clive?" Harriet asked.

"I don't know what he looks like."

"There's Geoff Banks." Harriet pointed to the farmer she'd met earlier. "We can ask him." She made her way through the gathering crowd.

Geoff headed away from the boat, and Harriet flagged him down. "What's going on?"

"A PLB has been activated around the south end of the bay."

"PLB?" Harriet asked.

"A personal locator beacon. It's a distress signal people can activate when they're in trouble."

"Why aren't you going out to find whoever it is?" Polly asked.

"They choose the crew best suited to the situation based on who answers the call. I'm not needed this time," Geoff explained.

"Is Clive here?" Harriet asked.

Geoff pressed his lips together. "No, sorry."

They watched the lifeboat head out into the bay. The sun wouldn't officially set for another hour, but it was already too low in the sky for them to see from the bottom of the cliffs, and the tide was going out. The lifeboat wouldn't be able to get too close to shore. Had someone misjudged the timing of the receding water and been cut off? Or were they swept out to sea with the fast-retreating tide?

They continued watching the shrinking lifeboat until it disappeared around the end of the bay, then they headed up the hill toward where Harriet had parked.

All of a sudden, Polly ducked her head and hooked her arm through Harriet's, making her do an about-face. "Those creepy blokes are back."

Harriet peeked over her shoulder. She couldn't tell for sure, given the dark sunglasses they didn't need in the waning light, but the men seemed to be looking their way. "Get in the middle of that group of tourists that's making their way up the hill," Harriet whispered.

"Polly, is that you?" a voice called.

Polly spun around. "Kevin? We were just on our way to the cricket pitch to find you."

A muscle-bound young man came over to them, flanked by three equally well-built friends. Harriet couldn't resist another glance at the creepy sunglass-dudes.

"We heard about the emergency call and came down to see if we could help," Kevin said. "Do you know what's going on?"

Polly filled them in and introduced Harriet. "We were hoping you could help us find someone we think works with the coast guard. Do you know a Clive Talbot?"

"Never heard of him." Kevin looked at the other guys. "Have you?"

Two of the three shook their heads, but the third nodded. "I've heard the name. A tall bloke came by the station a few days ago asking about him."

"Was it one of those guys?" Harriet pointed in the direction she'd last seen the two men who'd seemed to be following her and Polly, but they'd disappeared. "Never mind. They're gone. Did the guy say why he wanted Clive?"

"Not that I heard. When the receptionist told him she couldn't help him, he got belligerent, and I stepped in. He said it was important that he see Clive, but when I said I'd never heard of a Clive and maybe he should try another station, he finally got the message and left."

"Do you remember any identifying features about him?" Harriet pressed. The fact someone else was searching for Clive had to be significant. And if that someone had found him, it might explain why Clive hadn't responded to Aunt Jinny's messages.

"He was wearing sunglasses—I'll never understand people who wear those things inside—and he had a scar on his chin. Faint, mind you, but still there. When his sleeve slid up, I noticed a nasty scratch on his arm. You know, like from a cat or something."

Harriet's pulse spiked. Or from a woman trying to defend herself? But why would Rowena's captor want to find her husband? "What day was this? Do you remember?"

"I think it was Wednesday. Yeah, Wednesday."

Two days before Rowena's disappearance.

"Did you notice what kind of car the guy drove?" Polly asked.

"Sorry, I didn't follow him out."

"Does the coast guard station have cameras monitoring the lobby or parking area?" Harriet asked.

He shook his head.

"Okay." Anxious to get this newest information to Van, Harriet tugged on Polly's arm. "Thank you so much. We appreciate your help."

"You lasses want to join us for a game of darts?" Kevin asked.

"Maybe some other time." Polly looped her arm through Harriet's. "We're on a mission."

Kevin walked backward as he pressed his case. "What's this Clive chap have that I don't?"

"A baby who needs him."

That stopped Kevin cold. "Right. See you around." He hurried away with his friends.

Harriet chuckled at his abrupt departure. "You probably shouldn't have said that last part, since the police were adamant that word of Benji's abandonment not be leaked."

"I didn't mention his name," Polly said.

"But we did tell them his dad's name."

"That's true." Polly gazed around. "It might have been smart to ask them to escort us up to the carpark in case those blokes in the sunglasses show up again."

Harriet shuddered. "We'll stick close to the others heading up the hill. I'm sure those guys won't give us any trouble." At least she hoped they wouldn't.

"Do you think it's weird that the police are keeping everything under wraps?" Polly mused. "Van said it was so they 'could control the narrative,' but nothing about Rowena's disappearance has been in the news, and there were only a few lines about the stolen painting."

"That reminds me, I need to ask Mrs. Winslow to update the gallery's website that the unveiling has to be postponed. I probably should let Henderson's grandson know too, so he can get the word to his blog followers and—" Harriet stopped and smacked herself on the forehead. "I can't believe it never occurred to me to tell Van that Callum also knew where the painting was being held."

"You don't think he stole it, do you? If he wanted it, he would've contested the will, right?"

"It would've been the logical thing to do, but I don't think we should discount him."

"I'd like to know why the police haven't found Rowena's husband. They should be able to access tax records, phone records, bank records, or some other kind of record that would tell them where he works. Van said a detective talked to Rowena's neighbors, and they didn't seem to know much about the couple. Said they mostly kept to themselves and her husband was away a lot."

"And why was that man trying to find him?" Harriet winced at an uncomfortable new thought. "Maybe the police can't find out who Clive works for because his business dealings aren't exactly—well…"

"Legal?" Polly finished for her.

"I hate to put it that way, but think about it. It would certainly contribute to Rowena's postpartum depression. It's one thing to be married to a criminal, but it's another thing to bring a baby into the mix."

"And it would explain why they keep to themselves and why the police can't track him down," Polly added.

"As well as why the police want to control the narrative. If they're not sure whether Rowena's disappearance, or the painting's, is Clive's doing or the work of a rival."

"But if the police know Clive is a criminal, how could they let Jinny keep Benji, potentially putting all of us in danger?" Polly demanded.

A shudder went through Harriet. "Maybe he's not the violent type. He and Rowena certainly wouldn't want to endanger their baby."

"We hope, anyway."

Harriet's mouth went dry, as the image of the men from the Crow's Nest rose to her mind. "Did you happen to notice if either of those guys from the pub had a scar on his jaw or scratches on his arm?"

"I made a point *not* to study them. I didn't want them to think I was showing interest. You don't think they know we have Benji, do you? Or that they'll kidnap him to draw out his father?"

Harriet quickened her pace. "We'd better find Van and update him."

She groaned as her phone rang. Although the after-hours calls had decreased significantly since lambing season was finished, the biggest disadvantage of being a single-vet practice was being on call 24/7.

But at the sight of Aunt Jinny's name, Harriet's pulse jumped. She tapped the screen. "Aunt Jinny, what's wrong?"

"Harriet? Harriet?" Aunt Jinny's voice rose with each repetition of her name.

"Aunt Jinny, is Benji okay?"

The line went dead.

Harriet motioned Polly toward the passenger seat and tossed her the phone. "Try to get Aunt Jinny again. And if you can't, call emergency services." Harriet started the engine.

"What are you going to do?"

Harriet barreled onto the road. "Get us back to Cobble Hill. Now."

CHAPTER TWELVE

Harriet tightened her grip on the steering wheel as Polly reached Aunt Jinny on the phone and put her on speaker. "Jinny, what's going on?"

"Sorry, my reception is bad right now. You have to get to the vet clinic. Mrs. Huddersley's Yorkie was kicked by a stray cow. He has a nasty gash and is bleeding badly. I found her banging on the door, quite hysterical."

"Benji's okay?" Harriet verified.

"Yes. He's with us in the clinic."

"Oh, good. Good. We'll be there in five minutes." The call dropped again.

Harriet tamped down her frustration that their conversation with Van would have to wait but was grateful their panic had been misguided. Maybe their wild theories about the Talbots being criminals were as well.

She shook the thought from her head, needing to focus on the emergency awaiting her in the clinic. "Do you mind coming with me?" she asked Polly. "I may need a second pair of hands—if not with the Yorkie, then with keeping Mrs. Huddersley calm."

"No problem. I'll call Rand. Find out if he's aware of the situation." Rand Cromwell was the local dog catcher. Harriet was surprised, but assumed he must deal with more than stray dogs.

When Polly finished her call, she said, "Someone who saw the attack called Cromwell right away. Sounds like this isn't the first time this cow has been in trouble."

"Hopefully, the owners will do a better job of keeping her behind the fence from here on out."

By the time Harriet and Polly reached the clinic, Mrs. Huddersley was in the waiting room, entertaining Benji with the help of Charlie and Maxwell and enjoying a cup of tea. "Evening, Mrs. Huddersley. Is Dr. Garrett with Scooby?"

"Yes. I'm so sorry to drag you home so abruptly, but I didn't know where else to go. Thank goodness Dr. Garrett was here." Mrs. Huddersley's cheeks grew pink as she ducked her head. "I was in quite a state. But she tells me it looks much worse than it is."

Harriet gave the woman a reassuring smile. Aunt Jinny's bedside manner was top notch. "I'll see how she's doing, all right?" Harriet motioned Polly to join her.

They found Aunt Jinny in the exam room, attempting to clean the dog's wounds. "Oh, am I glad you're here. I think you're going to need to give Scooby a sedative to be able to do a proper job. He's going to need stitches."

Thanking her profusely, Harriet relieved Aunt Jinny of medical duties—and not a second too soon, as Benji's cries reached their ears. Aunt Jinny rushed from the room.

Polly held the dog still while Harriet examined him.

"You poor boy. I guess that big nasty cow wasn't having any of your backtalk." The last time the little dog had come in for his vaccinations, he'd had an air of self-importance and been super feisty. He would confront any animal that dared approach him by bouncing on his front paws and yapping. Harriet assumed he thought it made him appear scarier, or at least unafraid. But this time, his rival obviously called his bluff. "Don't you worry. We'll have you all better in no time."

Polly set to work cleaning the wounds the moment the sedative kicked in. "Lucky for us, Mrs. Huddersley had his hair cut short for the summer."

"That's for sure." The dog's short fur made it easier to see his injury and what needed to be done.

"I dated a nob once who had a Yorkie with hair cut the traditional way—parted down the middle of its back and hanging to the ground." Polly chuckled. "When my brother saw it, he said it reminded him of a giant caterpillar."

Harriet smiled. With their tan heads and dark saddle, Yorkies did kind of resemble an inverted woolly bear caterpillar. By the time they'd patched Scooby up and given him painkillers and antibiotics, Harriet's early morning and the stress of the day had caught up to her. "I think I'll need to wait until tomorrow to track down Van. I can hardly keep my eyes open."

"You go on to bed. I'll take this little one out to Mrs. Huddersley. I'm sure she won't mind giving me a ride back to my house. I'll lock up when we leave."

Harriet thanked her, told her good night, and then made her weary way to bed.

The next thing she knew, she woke to the sound of footsteps in the hall.

Harriet jackknifed out of bed, blinking in surprise at the morning light already sneaking past the edges of the window curtains. The sound that had awakened her drew closer to her bedroom door and then stopped. She grabbed her phone, but the screen remained dark. She'd been so tired last night that she'd forgotten to put it on the charger. Tugging on the nearest clothes at hand, she stared around her room. There had to be something here that she could use to defend herself.

Snatching the massive veterinary textbook from her nightstand, she stood to the side of the door with her back to the wall. She swallowed the fear storming through her chest and raised the textbook over her head.

The knock made her jump. "Harriet?" Aunt Jinny's voice filtered through the door. "You awake?"

Tears sprang to Harriet's eyes as her arms suddenly felt like jelly. She set the textbook back on the dresser and opened the door. "What are you doing here? Where's Benji?"

"With Polly in reception."

Harriet locked the door separating the clinic from her living quarters at night. Aunt Jinny, of course, had a spare key to the house in case of an emergency.

"Polly was worried about you. The Land Rover is here, but she couldn't find you outside or at my place, and you weren't answering your phone."

"I forgot to charge it. I guess I needed more sleep than I realized." Harriet pocketed her phone so she could take it downstairs to charge.

Leading the way down the hall, Aunt Jinny said, "Polly is in a right state, talking about some men in sunglasses coming after Benji?"

Harriet tripped over her own feet at the realization that both of their imaginations must have worked overtime during the night.

"I wouldn't be surprised if she's already called Van," Aunt Jinny added. "Do you know what she's talking about?"

Harriet braced a hand on the wall. "Yes. But what's she doing here on a Sunday morning?" She pinched her fingers at the throbbing in the middle of her forehead. "It is Sunday, isn't it?"

Aunt Jinny chuckled. "It is. And I don't know what brought her here. She's not making any sense."

Harriet resumed walking. "She might have news."

They found Polly in a bright floral sundress, hovering at the door between the house and the clinic with Benji tucked protectively in her arms. Her shoulders sagged in obvious relief at Harriet's appearance. "Don't ever scare me like that again!"

"I'm sorry. My phone died. Do you have news?"

"No, I came because I didn't want to miss hearing what Van had to say about our theory. I thought you'd have called him first thing."

"What theory?" Aunt Jinny asked.

"Let me get some coffee, and then we'll fill you in." Harriet brushed her fingers on Benji's cheek. "Good morning, little guy."

Charlie paced back and forth in front of Polly and the baby as if establishing a protective barrier. Maxwell whined from his bed in the corner, still waiting for one of them to attach his wheeled prosthesis for the day.

Harriet quickly took care of that and dished out food for the two animals before putting coffee on to brew.

Aunt Jinny took a seat at the kitchen table. "Will one of you please tell me what you're talking about?"

Harriet and Polly joined her at the table, and Harriet expounded on the theories she'd entertained since scratching the Reynolds brothers from her suspect list. She started with the one where Mr. and Mrs. Rucksack stole the painting and somehow whisked Rowena away so she couldn't report them. Then she explained the other one about Rowena's husband being a longtime criminal, which would explain why the police hadn't been able to trace an employer.

"That one would also explain her baby blues," Polly said. "Her husband's career choice might bother her now that there's a baby in the picture."

"Yes," Harriet agreed. "And perhaps when Rowena realized her husband was stealing the painting, she tried to stop him or—we don't know. There's a bunch of ways it could have gone down. We were thinking they might have double-crossed another pair of criminals, who then kidnapped Rowena as payback or to extort money from Clive."

"The two men in the dark sunglasses in the pub," Polly added.

"Are you talking about the pair who were here the other day?" asked a voice from the doorway. Doreen Danby was married to the farmer next door and was the best neighbor a person could ask for. Today, she carried a divine-smelling pie.

Harriet's mouth watered. "That wouldn't happen to be suitable breakfast fare, would it?"

At the exact same moment, Polly asked a far more pertinent question. "You saw the men in sunglasses *here*?"

"Yes, and maybe," Doreen responded, setting the pie on the table. To Harriet, she added, "This is bilberry pie, by the way. My girls picked them this morning."

"And here I'm just getting out of bed." Harriet laughed as she got up to get plates and forks. "Thank you, Doreen. This is exactly what the doctor ordered."

Aunt Jinny chuckled. "I think I would suggest a nutrient-dense breakfast."

Harriet grabbed a canister of whipped cream from the refrigerator. "This counts as a serving of dairy, right?" She squirted a dollop on the slice Doreen put on her plate then took a bite. "Perfect. Can I get you some coffee?"

Aunt Jinny planted her palms on the table and pushed back her chair. "I'll fix the coffee. You finish telling me what the deal is with the men in sunglasses."

"When, exactly, did you see them here?" Polly asked Doreen.

Doreen scrunched her face up in apparent thought. "Well, I don't know if they were the same men you're talking about. I just remember thinking it was strange because it wasn't a sunny day at all. It was Thursday—no, Friday. And it was after lunch, because I planned to make a shepherd's pie for dinner and walked over to see if Harriet wanted to see how I do it. But you were called out to an emergency."

"That fits the time frame," Polly blurted.

Doreen frowned. "Time frame for what?"

"My father's newly returned painting was stolen from the gallery," Aunt Jinny explained.

Doreen gasped. "I had no idea. I'm so sorry. Thommy said he saw a police car over here, but I assumed it was that young DC Worthington—" She looked at Polly and broke off.

Surprisingly, Doreen hadn't asked about the baby sleeping contentedly in Polly's arms. She likely knew Aunt Jinny occasionally offered emergency foster care.

"The police never questioned you?" Harriet asked.

"No." Doreen accepted a steaming mug of coffee from Aunt Jinny.

"How well did you see the men in sunglasses?" Polly asked. "Where were they? What were they doing? Did you see what car they drove?"

"I didn't pay them much mind to be honest." Doreen shook her head, clearly frustrated with herself. "I noticed them going up the driveway with a young woman between them. She seemed to be having difficulty walking, so I assumed they were helping her to her car. You know how the tourists have been parking up and down the road lately."

"I'm sorry," Harriet said. "I'm sure that's been inconvenient."

Doreen patted her hand. "Don't you worry. They don't bother us. I'm happy to see your grandfather's gallery is still so popular."

"Did you recognize the woman?" Polly pressed.

"No. She had her head down, and I couldn't see her face. I assumed they were all tourists. Do you think they could have been your thieves? It's so unsettling to think I might have seen them and done nothing."

Harriet exchanged glances with Polly and Aunt Jinny. They were practically sworn to secrecy regarding Rowena's disappearance. Harriet gritted her teeth. She hated to keep her neighbor in the dark after all the kindness Doreen had shown her.

"Did you notice them carrying anything that could have concealed a painting?" Aunt Jinny asked, buying Harriet time to think through how much to share with Doreen.

"Not that I noticed. Like I said, they caught my attention because it was such a cloudy day and they were wearing dark sunglasses. But I only glanced at them."

Another possibility flitted through Harriet's mind. If anyone would know of an entrance to the town's infamous smuggling tunnels, it would be Doreen. "It occurred to me that they might have slipped away unnoticed through a smuggling tunnel. Do you know of any entrances to them up here?"

Doreen leaned back in her chair, sipping her coffee. A smile played on her lips. "Before he passed, my father-in-law used to love to tell tales to our girls about his grandfather sneaking off through the tunnels into town. I got so worried my girls would do the same that I had Tom stop up the entrance."

Harriet's pulse quickened. "So there is an entrance around here?"

"Amid the ruins of one of the old barns, but the tunnels are centuries old. You'd be taking your life in your hands trying to get through."

"Criminals take risks all the time," Polly said. "Can you show us where it is?"

"If it's still sealed, at least then we can cross the theory off our list," Harriet added.

Doreen cocked her head. "You're playing detective on top of doctoring animals? Again?"

"I feel personally responsible for Grandad's painting," Harriet explained. "It's part of his legacy, and I'm its custodian, along with

Aunt Jinny. I want to chase down every lead I can think of until the painting is safely home."

"I can't say I fault that thinking." Doreen consulted her watch. "Church doesn't start for another couple hours, so I can take you now if you like. It's not far."

Harriet polished off her pie and coffee. "Let's go."

Aunt Jinny took Benji back from Polly. "Mind how you go. And keep me posted."

"Will do." Harriet grabbed her wellies then glanced at Polly's open-toed sandals. "Maybe you'd better wear these, and I'll get my hiking boots." She handed the rubber boots to Polly and fetched her other boots from the closet.

Outside, dark gray clouds piled up on the horizon like distant mountains, threatening to send heavy rain. Doreen led them across the pasture not far from the rear of the gallery, raising Harriet's hopes that this could be the route their thieves had taken. The grass was grazed too close to the ground and the ground too dry to tell whether anyone had recently gone that way.

"It's in here," Doreen said as they reached the stone ruins of a centuries-old barn. The roof had long ago collapsed, its rubble filling the space where animals would have once huddled to escape the elements. Doreen pushed aside a rotted beam and shook her head. "The trapdoor was in the corner there. Doesn't look as if this mess has been disturbed in years."

Harriet's hopes deflated along with her chest. "Okay. I suppose it was a long shot."

"When my mother had jewelry stolen years ago, the police told her the best chance of getting it back was to check at pawn shops and such. With a painting like your grandad's, perhaps checking with other art galleries and auction houses would give you a lead," Doreen suggested.

"I did call several of them," Polly said. "And Van said he would have it listed on a stolen-art database that brokers are supposed to check before acquiring new pieces."

"But thieves are more likely to sell to unscrupulous dealers whose customers aren't concerned about such things," Doreen said.

"I thought the same thing," Polly agreed.

"I'll be praying you find it." Doreen pointed to the sky. "You best hurry back now. The thunderstorm is rolling in quick."

Harriet and Polly rushed toward the clinic.

Alfie waved from where he was filling the boarding donkey's water trough with a hose. "Need a shower?" He aimed the hose at them, with his thumb over the end making it spray in a wide fan, though it didn't hit them.

Polly and Harriet laughed at his antics. He was an intelligent boy, and Harriet couldn't help but admire his sunny disposition and strong work ethic.

"What I was about to say before Alfie took to chasing us with a hose," Polly said as they continued walking, "is that just because those blokes didn't escape through a tunnel doesn't mean they didn't take the painting. And Rowena. You heard what Mrs. Danby said. The pair seemed to be 'helping' the woman walk." She held the door open for Harriet. "Maybe they had a gun to her ribs so she wouldn't scream. We have to tell Van."

"Would you be willing to call him and see if he can come around soon? I desperately need to shower and change before church."

"Will do."

"Great." Harriet toed off her boots. "I'll be as quick as I can. Make yourself at home."

Twenty minutes later, wearing a blue wrap dress and braiding her hair into one long plait, Harriet joined Polly in the kitchen once more. "Van's not here?"

"The officer who answered the phone said Van's unavailable this morning."

"I guess we'll have to wait to speak to him after church then."

Polly shifted one of Grandad's journals toward Harriet. "Did you know the Henderson farm, owned by the man your grandad did the missing painting for, was next door to Goose Beck Farm?"

Harriet scanned the entry. "This must have been what is now the Vails' place."

"Gilbert Vail added it to his holding. Your grandad describes him as 'ambitious.'"

Harriet frowned, wondering if Will's faith in the man's integrity might be unfounded after all.

"Apparently, Mr. Staveley wanted to buy the place too, so Henderson planned to sell everything at public auction. But Gilbert swooped in and convinced him to accept a cash offer that would save him the commission."

"That might explain the rumored bad blood between the neighbors." Harriet read the entry more carefully. "Grandad says Gilbert made Henderson a generous offer. That says something about his character."

Polly snorted. "Or his pocketbook. He could be the kind of guy who thinks he should be able to buy whatever he wants."

"And now he wants Goose Beck Farm," Harriet murmured.

"Exactly. So if Mr. Staveley won't sell it, what might Gilbert be willing to do to change his mind?"

"Have you been listening to the rumor mill?"

"Never." Polly sounded offended by the idea. And the fact that she was the second person to float the theory in as many days made it difficult for Harriet to dismiss the possibility as easily as Will had.

He'd said she cared more about the animals' welfare than of what Ned Staveley thought about her, but would Will see it that way if she questioned his opinion on Gilbert Vail's character?

CHAPTER THIRTEEN

For the first few minutes of the morning service, the rich music of the ancient pipe organ combined with the spirited voices of the choir and drowned out the theories chasing one another around Harriet's head. A shaft of sunlight even found a fissure in the thunderheads and slanted through the stained glass window, intensifying the gorgeous colors in the scene of Jesus carrying the once-lost lamb on His shoulders.

Rather than having pews or chairs arranged in rows that faced a platform at the front of the church, White Church had a three-tiered platform where the pastor stood to deliver his sermon, with walled family boxes, complete with pews and little doors, and more rows of benches on the balcony above.

Harriet invited Polly to join her and Aunt Jinny along with Jinny's son, Anthony, his wife, Olivia, and their six-year-old twins, Sebastian and Sophie, with Sophie delighting in holding Benji under Aunt Jinny's watchful hovering.

When Will offered prayers for the needs of the flock, he asked that all who were lost might be found, and she wondered if he was thinking of Benji's parents. After that, mulling over potential suspects and scenarios that could account for Rowena's disappearance stole her concentration.

Then Will read the twenty-eighth chapter of the book of Job, and the opening verses diverted Harriet's mind from its wandering. "'There is a mine for silver and a place where gold is refined. Iron is taken from the earth, and copper is smelted from ore.'"

Harriet leaned closer to her cousin, an idea percolating in the back of her mind. "Are there any mines around here?"

Anthony blinked, clearly surprised by the question. "Uh, there used to be an alum mine, but that closed in the late 1800s."

Harriet frowned, not familiar with alum mining—or specifically the kind of residual contamination it might leave behind that the Staveley cows could have picked up, possibly as runoff in a stream where they drank. But if the mine had closed so long ago, wouldn't they have seen the effects on the cattle before now?

"There were lots of collieries too. Coal mines. All through Yorkshire, they were," Olivia whispered. "But they started closing in the 1980s. It's been ten years now since the last one closed."

Harriet might be onto something with this theory after all, because being closed didn't mean the contamination stopped. The negative impact on water supplies from coal mining was well-documented. She knew she shouldn't, but she surreptitiously did an internet search on her smartphone to confirm that.

Anthony glanced at her phone. "Lead was mined in the Yorkshire Dales all the way back to Roman times."

"Isn't there a potash mine still operating near Whitby?" Polly whispered.

Aunt Jinny shushed them all, redirecting their focus to Pastor Will. He was explaining how the passage from Job used mining as an analogy for searching for wisdom. "There are so many things we don't know, that we can't see or seem to understand. And faith is trusting that God knows, that God sees, and that He understands."

Harriet squeezed her eyes shut and did something she should have done more deliberately from the outset—prayed for wisdom and guidance to find the answers that would allow her to help Benji and the animals in her care.

"So, how do we get that wisdom?" Will asked, almost as if he'd heard her prayer. "Proverbs tells us that the fear of the Lord is the beginning of wisdom."

Harriet sighed, knowing it was true, but also knowing she couldn't acquire wisdom by typing a few keywords into an online search engine.

Will went on to explain that believers had no reason to be afraid of God. "For a Christian, 'fear' refers to our awe of what He's done for us and what He is capable of doing, which motivates us to surrender to His will."

Harriet was still mulling over his words when people around her stirred to leave. She'd often seen God's hand at work in her life, even when things didn't go the way she hoped or planned, like when Dustin had broken off their engagement. If he hadn't, she might have opted to sell Cobble Hill and pocket the money rather than start a new chapter here. Now she couldn't imagine going back.

"You coming?" Polly asked.

Harriet straightened. As long as her patients had life, there was hope. She still wasn't sure she could save them, if indeed they had ingested the harmful byproducts of mining, as she had begun to fear. But if she found the source, she could work to see that the remaining herd and future offspring wouldn't face the same fate.

Polly searched her face. "You've had an epiphany, haven't you?"

"I think so. Mr. Staveley's cows show symptoms of lead poisoning, but until the blood results come in—whenever that is—I can't be sure, especially since we haven't found a potential source."

"But you're thinking mining could be the source?"

"Yes. I need to go home and do some research on where the mines were located and which way the water surrounding Goose Beck Farm flows. Who do you call in the UK if you want water tested for contaminants?"

"I'm not sure. But I can find out."

"Thank you. While we wait on results, I'm going to suggest to Mr. Staveley that we give all his cows injections to mitigate the effects of lead poisoning on the central nervous system, in case any of them have been exposed and aren't showing symptoms yet." She winced at the thought that it was possible that some might never exhibit symptoms but could have high enough levels to be considered unsafe for human consumption. "I'll also suggest he treat them with something to help reduce lead absorption. Neither will do a healthy cow any harm, but they may save one that's ingested poison."

"What about the cows that are already sick?"

"If it's lead poisoning, the concentrations in their tissue might already be too high for safe consumption. At this point I'm just hoping we can save the herd without cutting into the family's bottom line."

Aunt Jinny hurried back to where Harriet still stood with Polly. "Anthony has invited Benji and me over for lunch. Did you want to come?"

"I can't today. We're expecting Van to come by the farm." Harriet glanced around and lowered her voice. "We still need to tell him about our theories. We had one more that we didn't share with you, Aunt Jinny."

"Well, don't hold out on me now." Aunt Jinny held up a finger to Anthony to signal she'd be another minute.

"It's about Callum Henderson-Grainger. He knew where Grandad's painting was held. But I don't know if he was at the farm on Friday. He's not high on my suspect list, but I figured we should see if he has an alibi before ruling him out."

"I'm eager to know if the police have come up with any clues," Aunt Jinny said.

"I'll keep you posted," Harriet assured her.

At the church door, Will greeted Harriet at the end of the line of parishioners filing out. "Any news?"

"A theory, but that's all." She looked around, and since everyone except Polly had already moved on, Harriet asked, "How well do you know Rowena and Clive?"

"Not well, I'm afraid. Rowena has attended a few times when her husband has been away. But never with Clive."

"So, you haven't met him?"

"I did once when I visited their home. He struck me as very intelligent—much more knowledgeable of world events than most folks in Yorkshire."

"How do you mean?"

Smile lines creased the corners of Will's eyes. "Being a minister, I tend to watch world events rather closely, in case something happens that I feel I need to address in my next sermon. Having heard that Clive served in the navy, I was curious about his take on current events."

"And?"

"Like I said, he was extremely knowledgeable. Knew far more than I was aware of."

"We're not sure he was in the navy." Harriet shared their theory that he was a criminal, that Rowena wanted him to leave the business, and that maybe his partners or his enemies had kidnapped her.

Will scratched his chin as he mulled over their theory. "I guess it's possible, but it sounds a little far-fetched to me."

"Hopefully, we'll know better after we speak to Van," Polly chimed in. "Maybe he's heard whether the detectives were able to track down Clive's employer."

"I thought Clive worked for the coast guard?"

"I have a friend in the coast guard, and he's never heard of him."

Will shrugged. "Clive could have an administrative role or something. That would explain his frequent traveling."

Harriet frowned. She didn't know enough about how His Majesty's Coastguard operated to know if that was true, whereas their criminal theory seemed to plug all the holes.

"Well, if you need more help detecting, let me know," Will said.

"You're welcome to come to the farm now for our meeting with Van," Polly piped up.

"I'm afraid I can't today," Will said. "I've already accepted another lunch invitation."

"Your loss." Polly cheekily winked at Harriet.

Harriet ignored her friend and hoped her face wasn't as red as it felt.

As they headed toward Polly's car, Harriet spotted Geoff Banks and flagged him down. "Hey, did you hear how the lifeboat rescue went?"

"False alarm. A member of the coast guard team located the person on a footpath. His PLB was triggered accidentally. The lifeboat crew returned to shore without engaging."

"Do you get a lot of false alarms?"

"I had a case where a dog fell into the water from the top of the cliff, but he ended up rescuing himself before we arrived. And sometimes we're called out in case our assistance will be needed, like last week, when they had to do a helicopter rescue of a kid who was rock climbing."

Harriet's gaze strayed to a line of boats bobbing at anchor offshore at high tide. Cobble Hill Farm wasn't far from the cliff's edge. If a thief had an accomplice down below, he could have dropped the painting to a waiting boat in no time. But the more she considered it, the more it seemed too risky. Between ramblers walking the cliff trail and fishing boats and pleasure crafts in the water, the chance of being seen would've been too great. "Have you had any incidents involving smugglers lately?"

"They're often rescuing people being smuggled in across the English Channel, but nothing like that around here."

"My dad told us about that. A church down south is trying to help refugees find work and housing," Polly said.

"Thanks for the update, Geoff," Harriet said.

"Sure thing."

As they drove back to Cobble Hill Farm together, Polly asked Harriet, "Do you think the illegal channel crossings would be a reason a coast guard employee would be gone from home a lot? Living so far north and having to travel to the English Channel to deal with it, I mean."

"Are you talking about Clive? I thought we concluded he didn't work for the coast guard." Harriet sighed. Given the peculiar behavior Doreen had witnessed with the two men in sunglasses, the possibility Clive was mixed up with bad guys seemed the most logical theory.

Would Van think their criminal theory was a stretch? Police could only act on hard evidence. Then again, a good hunch might lead them to that evidence.

"If we find the painting—"

"We find the thief," Harriet finished.

"Or whoever the thief sold it to, who should be able to identify him. Someone like a pawn-shop broker, like Doreen suggested." Polly brightened as they started up the driveway at Cobble Hill. "Speaking of secondhand shopping, there's a giant car boot sale in Skirlington today. Maybe we should go check it out. It started at six this morning, so we might already be too late. I wish I'd thought of it sooner. We could've staked it out to scout for the painting."

"Skirlington? Where's that?"

"On the coast south of here." Polly made a face. "It's almost an hour and a half drive. No way we can make it in time now. But there's another one in Strawberry Fields in Bridlington on Thursdays. That's only an hour away."

"Except we have clinic hours that day."

"I could ask my mom to scout it out. She loves boot sales."

"Let's see what Van thinks first. I wouldn't want her to confront a criminal and get into worse trouble than Rowena."

The storm that had threatened all morning had blown past, leaving beautiful blue skies in its wake. Charlie met them at the car when they stepped out, meowing loudly.

"I think she's put out that she can't find Benji," Polly speculated.

Harriet lifted the cat and scratched her furry head. "You're such a good girl. Don't you worry. The baby is in safe hands with Aunt Jinny."

Charlie's continued yowls suggested she wasn't convinced.

They went inside and fixed grilled cheese sandwiches and tea for lunch then carried them out to the garden to enjoy, where Maxwell could happily trundle around and still be with them.

They were about to have dessert when Van drove up. But he wasn't driving a police cruiser or wearing his uniform.

"You're just in time for a treat," Harriet told him when he got out of his car. "It's Doreen's bilberry pie."

"That sounds perfect. Thanks."

As Harriet gathered their lunch plates, Polly motioned to Van's clothes. "Not working today?"

He grinned. "I wasn't scheduled. But I went undercover."

Harriet's heart jumped to her throat. "Did you find Rowena or Grandad's painting?"

The question wiped the grin from his face. "Sorry, no. I scoured the boot sale in Skirlington for three hours. But nothing."

Something akin to admiration lit Polly's expression. "I was telling Harriet that I wished I'd thought to do that this morning. It was nice of you to drive all that way to do that on your own time."

The familiar blush, never far away when Polly was near, colored Van's cheeks. "I know how important the painting is to the doc for sentimental reasons. And you can't put a price on finding someone."

"No you can't," Polly agreed. She beckoned him to take a seat at the bistro table, and Harriet left to go to the kitchen.

When she returned a few minutes later with a tray of desserts and a fresh pot of tea, the pair were totally absorbed in conversation.

"Harriet," Polly exclaimed, "Van thinks we might be onto something with our theory about Clive being a criminal."

Van gratefully accepted a piece of pie and cup of tea. "I'll mention it when I meet with DI McCormick in the morning."

"Van was just telling me they've eliminated Callum Henderson-Grainger as a suspect," Polly added.

"Mrs. Winslow mentioned the blog he did on the painting, but he has an ironclad alibi," Van explained. "He was hosting a live video event at a festival forty miles away all last week."

"I'm relieved to hear it." Harriet hadn't wanted to believe Callum was capable of sneaking back to steal the painting when he'd seemed so genuine during their interview. She asked about Mr. and Mrs. Rucksack.

Van frowned. "This is the first I'm hearing about them. I'll try to track them down at the rentals in town."

"I know they didn't have accommodations arranged when they first arrived, because they tried to get a place at the caravan park."

"Then they might have had to push on to another town in the area. I'll mention them to the DI too."

Harriet appreciated his willingness to entertain their theories and his commitment to leaving no stone unturned. "Since I have another mystery on my hands, I'll leave you two to visit, so I can research mining in Yorkshire," she said. "Unless you happen to know anything about potential contamination of the waterways or pastures around here from old mines."

"Never heard tell of anything like that," Van replied.

Harriet stifled a sigh. "I'm not sure it's the case. But right now, it's the best explanation I can think of for the symptoms I'm seeing in Mr. Staveley's cattle." Short of Gilbert Vail deliberately poisoning them.

"That I have heard of," Van admitted. "There's been a lot of grumbling among the farmers about the Yank who quarantined his farm."

Terrific. Between her professional reputation being in jeopardy over her handling of the Staveley situation and the public relations nightmare if word got out that a woman had disappeared from Cobble Hill Farm, Harriet's new career in the UK might be over before it really got started.

CHAPTER FOURTEEN

By late Sunday afternoon, after a couple of hours scouring the internet, Harriet still had no compelling proof that the Staveley cows had been exposed to contamination from mining operations. But her instincts told her they had lead poisoning. And if the rest of his cows had also encountered the source, the sooner they started treatments, the better their chances of avoiding the poison reaching dangerous levels in their systems.

She decided that if he was going to balk at her idea, she would rather challenge him face-to-face than try to reason with him over the phone. She collected enough supplies to treat the entire herd and loaded them into the Land Rover.

Halfway there, a call came in on her phone. Although she could answer it hands-free, she stopped at the side of the road, anticipating that she might need to make a note of an address.

"Gilbert Vail here," the caller announced. "I've got a sick cow. Can you come out?"

Her heart pummeled her ribs. "I'll be right there." She pulled back onto the road and picked up speed. If this cow exhibited the same symptoms as Mr. Staveley's, that would pretty well eliminate the possibility that he'd poisoned his neighbor's herd. Of course, his cow could be sick with any number of unrelated illnesses. It was his clipped tone and the fact he shared grazing land with the Staveleys that made her suspect it would be the same ailment that was afflicting the Staveleys' animals. Then again, Yorkshire farmers tended to sound brusque most of the time.

When she drove up his driveway, Gilbert emerged from his house, still tugging on his wellingtons. "You made it here right quick."

"I was in the area." She grabbed her bag from the vehicle. "Where's your cow?"

"It's a calf. I penned him and his mother up behind the barn."

The instant she saw the calf, she knew it was the same thing Mr. Staveley's cows had, and the self-doubts stampeded through her mind. What if she was wrong and it wasn't poison? As logical as the mine theory sounded, she hadn't been able to find any evidence of one close enough to be a likely source. She tamped down the doubts and gave the calf a thorough going-over to ensure she wasn't merely seeing what she'd expected to see.

"I'm afraid your calf is exhibiting the same symptoms as several of the Staveley stock. I'll need to take a blood test to confirm the diagnosis. But I believe we have a case of lead poisoning." She explained her reasoning, as well as the recommended treatments. "Lab results can take up to a week. But if they've all been exposed to lead, acting now might save you from greater loss."

Although he was adamant that no one had been fool enough to leave anything dangerous lying around for the cattle to access, Gilbert agreed to administer the preventative treatments, and Harriet left him with supplies to dose his entire herd, leaving herself with enough to do the same for Mr. Staveley.

Gilbert vigorously shook her hand, his voice and face betraying the emotional toll worry had clearly already taken on him. These Yorkshire farmers might act as hard as nails on the outside, but their concern for their animals ran deep.

Next stop, she caught Mr. Staveley as he was heading in for Sunday dinner. To her surprise, he didn't seem perturbed by her presuming to come unannounced. In fact, he sounded grateful and readily agreed to the treatments.

Since he was more than capable of administering the injections himself, she left him with the necessary supplies. "Please let me know if you notice any changes one way or the other. And I'll be in touch again as soon as we get the lab results on the blood test."

"Will do, lass."

As she drove home, her heart felt lighter than it had in days. She hadn't cured the cows, but she'd settled on a proactive course that might buy them the time their bodies needed to expel the toxin.

The wispy clouds on the western horizon gleamed a brilliant crimson. The old weather adage "Red sky at night, sailor's delight," drifted through her thoughts. She prayed tomorrow would be equally bright for Mr. Staveley and Gilbert when they inspected their stock once more.

As she climbed out of the Land Rover back at Cobble Hill Farm, she spotted Aunt Jinny's silhouette in an upstairs window, cradling the baby. "Now if only we could figure out what happened to your mama," she whispered.

The next day, her farm calls began two hours before Polly was scheduled to arrive at the clinic. Satisfaction filled her at the sight of a busy schedule for the day.

Her first stop was to treat a pet sheep named Bo Peep who was off her feed.

Her owner, Felicity Barnes, stood outside the pen, watching Harriet's every move with open anxiety.

After shedding her lightweight sweater, Harriet examined the sheep then asked to see her food. She offered some to Bo Peep, who turned up her nose. Harriet grinned. "You'll be happy to know nothing is wrong with her health. She's simply decided she doesn't like the mix of grains in her current batch of food. Try switching it up. You'll land on something she'll go for." She listed a few changes to try.

Felicity's expression cleared. "Really? That's it?"

Grateful for an easy fix for once, Harriet chuckled. "Yes, that's really it. Sheep can be picky eaters. You're taking excellent care of this one. She's at a good weight and clearly in peak health. It doesn't surprise me at all that she's developed a bit of a diva attitude. We'll have her back to her old self in no time."

As Harriet gathered her bag to leave, she couldn't find her sweater. "Did you move my sweater—sorry, my jumper?" she asked Felicity.

Felicity gnawed her bottom lip. "Oh dear. Esther," she called to her daughter, "go find Billy."

A minute later, they heard the girl behind the barn scolding Billy. When Felicity ran to intervene, Harriet followed a few steps behind, thinking Billy must be Esther's younger brother, who was perhaps a prankster. Not having any brothers, Harriet didn't know from personal experience, but Polly had said her brothers had often teased her and her friends when they were little, hiding their dolls and such.

Harriet rounded the barn and faltered at the sight of a goat—whose name was apparently Billy—playing tug-of-war with her sweater.

"I'm so sorry. He's a cheeky little rascal." Felicity took over Esther's end of the tug-of-war game and offered the goat a treat in her other hand that convinced him to let go. Holding the sweater against her chest, Felicity apologized profusely. "I'll wash it for you and then get it back to you."

"That's not necessary." Harriet relieved her of the sweater with a smile. "I've seen much worse, but I'll keep that bribery technique in mind."

"It never fails." Felicity winked. "Thank you so much for everything. I'll make up the jumper to you. Don't leave yet." She jogged toward her house and called over her shoulder, "I'll meet you at your vehicle."

A few minutes later, Harriet set out for her next call with the aroma of fresh-baked coconut currant buns swirling through the Land Rover.

Next on her list was a regular checkup on a donkey. Although donkeys were rarely the most cooperative of patients, Eli stood patiently while she poked and prodded him. She updated his vaccinations and handed the appropriate paperwork to the farmer.

"Wow, you don't let the grass grow under your feet, do you?" he asked, sounding duly impressed.

"It helps that you have a good-tempered donkey." Grinning, she packed away her supplies. The farmer's admiration gave her a much-needed confidence boost. It was the kind of response she longed to elicit from the likes of Mr. Staveley. She'd let herself hope last night that she'd made a little headway in that direction, but the fact he hadn't called with a status update yet made her wonder if he'd done as she'd suggested.

She'd known owning a vet practice wouldn't be easy and had even anticipated that some of the older farmers might take a while to warm up to her. She'd faced similar skepticism about her abilities in her first months stateside as a newly qualified vet making farm calls on her own.

The outright refusal of Yorkshire farmers to even consider availing themselves of her services, however, was harder to take. Especially from those who'd used the practice when her grandfather had owned it. In fact, now that one of the most prominent of them had finally called her in on a case, part of her had to wonder if it was merely to validate his negative opinion of her abilities if she failed to save his animals.

Accepting an invitation to stay for tea and biscuits, Harriet packed her supplies back into her vehicle in case she was called to an emergency. Then she enjoyed a chat with the farmer, Joe, and his daughter, Erin.

"I hear you've had some dealings with our pinder," Joe said.

"Pinder?" In the months since she'd arrived in Yorkshire, she'd learned quite a few novel expressions, but pinder was a new one.

"Rand Cromwell."

"Oh yes, the dog catcher. I hadn't heard him called a pinder."

Joe chuckled. "That's what the person who dealt with wayward animals was called in the old days." He pointed up the road to a small area hemmed in by stone walls within the larger walled field. "That there's the original pinder yard from the 1600s."

"That's amazing."

"Aye. The pinder would pen any sheep or cattle found wandering the roads, and their owner would have to pay a shilling to get them back."

"Remind me how much that is again."

"That's the old money system. Twenty shillings to a pound."

"Okay, so about five pence?"

"A shilling was divided into twelve pence."

Harriet chuckled. "Well, that couldn't have been easy."

Joe laughed.

"Until they switched to the decimal system in 1971, there were 240 pennies in a pound," Erin explained. "I'm glad it happened before I was born."

"For sure," Harriet agreed. "The decimal system is so much easier to understand. Although I imagine Rand fines more than five pence these days. Not that I suppose he deals much with wayward farm animals anymore." Although she supposed Scooby's owner would probably call for his services soon if she hadn't already.

"He gets called by townies if farm animals wander into their gardens," Joe said.

"For a while, a hobby farm on the edge of town had a goat that was a brilliant escape artist," Erin added. "He had a penchant for nibbling on the neighbor's wash hanging out."

"They called the pinder to collect the goat more than a few times when its owners were out at their day jobs," Joe added with a laugh.

Harriet grinned, pretty sure she'd met the culprit earlier that day.

After leaving Joe's farm, Harriet stopped at the preserved pinder yard and read the historical plaque marking the location.

The sight of the trodden grass around the walls, no doubt the work of tourists, reminded her of the cage-size depression Will had spotted on a similar roadside where the Reynolds brothers had stopped. She remembered that it was illegal for them to release the gray squirrels into the wild because their introduction to the UK in the late 1800s nearly wiped out the indigenous red squirrel.

The thought struck her like lightning. What if she was dealing with a similar cross-species virus infecting the Staveley cattle and not a case of poisoning at all?

Plenty of bats were in the area. And bats were notorious for carrying viruses. If one had died in the pasture and contaminated the cattle's water supply or fodder, they could have caught something that way. She'd seen it in Connecticut with a bird carcass in the silage. Except that had resulted in sudden death due to botulism.

She raked her eyes over the fields that, despite their beauty, could harbor such potential dangers. In fact, records of cross-species infection dated as far back as biblical times. Then again, the normal temperatures of Mr. Staveley's cattle had caused her to dismiss the likelihood of a virus. Nevertheless, it wouldn't hurt to pay him another visit and collect a few more vials of blood to see if she could spot anything under a microscope.

Grandad didn't have an electron microscope like the clinic where she'd worked stateside, so she wouldn't be able to see viruses. But examining the blood might give her another clue to go on while they waited for the lab results. Viruses caused documented changes that would be visible under the microscope, even if the virus itself wasn't.

She grabbed her phone and called Dr. Barry Tweedy before she could second-guess the impulse. Barry was a kind man in his mid-fifties who'd seen his share of mysterious ailments over the decades.

He picked up on the first ring. After rushing through the expected niceties, Harriet floated her theory that her clients' cows might have a cross-species infection.

When she finished, he was quiet for a long while. At last, he said, "It's a solid theory, but my advice is to wait on the lab results. Without those or an obvious source of infection, there's little you can do but treat the symptoms. As I said in my text, I haven't seen any comparable outbreak among my clients' farms. Like you, my first thought was poisoning."

Harriet thanked him for his time and tried Dr. Gavin Witty next but got his voice mail. She opted not to leave a message.

Barry had been hesitant to jump on board with her theory. Was she reaching? She prided herself on not doing that, especially in diagnostics. The last thing she needed was a reputation for not being knowledgeable and grasping at straws.

But like Will said, it didn't matter what people thought. She had been hired to care for the cattle. And their welfare had to come before any petty fear about how she was perceived by her colleagues or clients. She was investigating. That meant having the courage to follow up on every possibility, no matter how far-fetched, until she found the answer.

She climbed back into her vehicle and headed toward Goose Beck Farm.

CHAPTER FIFTEEN

arriet returned home with the samples minutes before her first office appointment. Rather than pass waiting clients, she slipped into the house through the side door after parking. She changed into fresh scrubs then grabbed a quick glass of water and an energy bar before entering the clinic.

"Any word from Van?" Harriet whispered to Polly as she paused at the reception desk to collect her first file.

Polly put a finger to her lips then led Harriet into an empty exam room and shut the door. "Not that he's sharing."

With all the secrecy, Harriet had expected some kind of development. "That's not like him."

"Tell me about it," Polly grumbled. "He asked me to make a list of everyone who came to the clinic on Friday, and Moira has to do the same for Dr. Garrett. I guess they're widening the net in their hunt for suspects."

"What about the sunglass-wearing guys and the rucksack couple? They're far more likely suspects than patients who didn't go anywhere near the gallery."

Polly shrugged. "Since the police are keeping such a tight lid on Rowena's disappearance, maybe Van is hoping someone saw something they didn't realize is important."

"I suppose." Harriet hooked her stethoscope around her neck and reached for the doorknob to call her first patient.

"Except," Polly said, stopping her with a hand on her arm, "I got the feeling his higher-ups ordered him to give us busywork because they don't want us interfering."

"Van wouldn't do that. Would he?"

"He wouldn't want to rub his superiors the wrong way. He knows we want to help, but he has to follow orders."

Harriet chewed on her bottom lip. "From my perspective, every day they take to return that baby to his mother and father is one day too long. So anything we can think of to expedite the search seems worth doing to me. It's not just because I want my grandfather's painting recovered."

"I know. I've seen the way you look at Benji."

Harriet felt her face heat. She hadn't realized the feelings the infant stirred in her had been so obvious. "Have you already given Van our clients' names?"

"Not yet."

"Well, maybe you could call each of them first to let them know he might contact them."

"And if they happen to mention to me what they would tell him?"

Harriet smiled. "A little casual conversation would only be natural. And if Van complains, we can remind him that we need to respect our clients' privacy. So if we were going to give him names, we needed to notify them first." She mentally ran through the names of the patients she'd had Friday morning, confident Polly wouldn't be tipping off a kidnapping thief.

Polly chuckled. "Good plan. I'll get right on those calls."

The day passed in a blur. When she walked the last scheduled patient and client back to reception, she found Polly making a fuss over Benji.

The client, Mr. Bellingham, stared at the baby. "Did you call him Benji? Is that the Talbot baby?"

Aunt Jinny shot Harriet a worried glance before responding in a somewhat shaky voice, "Yes. I'm watching him for a few days."

The man's shoulders sagged in apparent relief. "So his mum's not in trouble then?"

"Why would you think that?" Harriet asked.

"Because their cat has been coming to our house since Friday afternoon, when Rowena didn't come home at lunchtime. When she still wasn't home by Saturday morning, I called the police. I was afraid this fella's mum was in an accident or something." He shot Aunt Jinny a sheepish grin, and Harriet wondered if he'd noticed Rowena's baby blues too. "Or that her husband was. I suspect his job is dangerous. I saw a nasty scar on his arm once, possibly from a recent gunshot wound. Anyway, it wasn't like Rowena to leave without making arrangements for the cat."

Aunt Jinny held Benji closer. "And what did DC Worthington tell you when you called the police?"

Mr. Bellingham's forehead furrowed. "It wasn't him." He dug a business card out of his wallet and passed it to Aunt Jinny. "It was a Detective Ascot."

Aunt Jinny skimmed the card, her eyes widening, then handed it to Harriet.

Harriet blinked at the sight of the agency on the card. Why hadn't Van told them that the regional crime squad was handling the investigation into Rowena's disappearance? "And what did Detective Ascot tell you?"

"Not to worry. That she and her husband were suddenly called out of town. He might've said for a family emergency." The man scratched his head as if he might draw out the memory that way. "No, that's what my wife figured. But this Ascot fella told us that Clive appreciated us taking care of their cat until they got back."

Harriet gaped. "Detective Ascot said he'd actually talked to Clive? Clive Talbot?"

"He did."

What on earth was going on? Had the detective lied to Mr. Bellingham to contain the news? Because if the police were in contact with Clive, why hadn't he come for Benji? Or at least called Aunt Jinny to check in on him?

Mr. Bellingham glanced at his watch. "Sorry, I need to get this bill settled. My wife warned me not to dally. Our grandson has a football match tonight."

As Polly processed his payment for his English spaniel's annual checkup, Aunt Jinny drew Harriet aside. "I think we need to call this Detective Ascot and find out what's going on."

"I'm not sure that's the best idea. Polly got the impression this morning that Van's stonewalling us, which isn't like him at all. I figure it's got to be on orders from higher up. If we can coax answers out of anyone, it's most likely to be Van."

Benji started fussing, and Aunt Jinny bounced him until he quieted. "Okay, do you think you can get him over here? We'll have a better chance of getting the information out of him in person."

"No problem." Harriet grinned. "I'll have Polly ask him to come."

They said goodbye to Mr. Bellingham as he left with his dog, and then Harriet enlisted Polly to call Van. Less than a minute later, Polly yanked her phone away from her ear and stared at the screen. "I think he just rejected my call."

"It didn't go to voice mail?" Harriet asked.

"No, it stopped ringing."

Harriet wondered if Van had just hurt his chances with Polly. She did not sound at all impressed.

Polly's phone dinged with a text message alert. "It's from Van. 'Sorry, I'm in a meeting. Will call when I can.'"

"Okay, I guess we wait then." Harriet headed for the fridge to get the samples she'd collected that morning. "In the meantime, I have some more investigating to do for a client."

"And I'd better get home and feed this little guy," Aunt Jinny said.

"Wait a minute," Polly said. "Is Rowena's husband your patient too?"

Aunt Jinny hesitated.

"Well?" Polly prodded. "If you're not his doctor, who else would he go to?"

Aunt Jinny shrugged. "If he works for the coast guard or the rescue team in another town, perhaps he has a doctor there. Or maybe he hasn't been sick since they've moved here."

"So you never saw the wound Mr. Bellingham mentioned?"

"No."

"Sounds a little suspicious, don't you think? A friend of mine works in the coast guard, and he's never been shot."

"Didn't someone say Clive was former navy?" Aunt Jinny asked. "He could've been shot then."

Polly shook her head. "Mr. Bellingham made a point of saying the scar wasn't that old."

"Perhaps, but it's not always easy to tell."

"If Clive was shot in the not-so-distant past," Harriet said, "it would fit our theory that he's a criminal whose wife was targeted by someone he double-crossed."

"Every time I met him when he accompanied Rowena to her appointments and at the baby's delivery, he seemed like a nice man," Aunt Jinny said. "He never struck me as someone with enemies."

"But a good criminal could con anyone, right?" Polly pressed.

Benji burst into tears, as if he knew she'd said something mean about his father.

Aunt Jinny snuggled Benji to her chest. "There, there. Don't you listen to Miss Polly." To Polly, she added, "I hope for this little guy's sake that your theory is wrong."

"Me too, but we're running out of possibilities," Polly said.

"Pray we find out soon. I'll talk to you later."

The instant Aunt Jinny opened the door, Charlie dashed in, apparently attuned to Benji's distress.

Harriet caught the cat to prevent her from following the pair back to the dower cottage. "It's okay. The baby's fine."

Charlie yowled, clearly wanting to make that determination for herself.

Polly started tidying the reception area. "After you're done with the investigation you talked about, would you like to go into town with me for dinner? We could keep our eyes peeled for the rucksack couple and the blokes with the sunglasses. Maybe have Van meet us somewhere."

"I love that idea." Harriet motioned to the supply room that doubled as a lab. "Can you give me half an hour?"

"No problem."

When Harriet reemerged from the lab, she hadn't gained any new insight into the cows' condition. Their red blood cell count seemed low, which was consistent with lead poisoning but also with numerous other conditions. Unfortunately, the earliest she would likely get results back from the lab was Wednesday.

Polly closed one of Grandad's journals. "Did you know Doc Bailey treated a military working dog that served in the Falkland Islands War, as well as a German shepherd that served as a spy in Iraq?"

Harriet smiled. "No, I didn't know that. What does he write about the dogs?"

"The military working dog was a Belgian Malinois named Sprinter. He helped locate downed airmen in the Falklands. The German shepherd was named Kim after a British spy, Kim Philby. The dog parachuted into Iraq with his handler and was sent to find enemy hideouts with a tiny camera attached to his head that beamed live images back to the troops to alert them to ambushes and such."

"Wow, I can't believe I never heard that story from Grandad."

"Maybe he wasn't at liberty to share the information," Polly joked.

Harriet rolled her eyes. "Grandad wasn't a spy."

"How can you be sure? I heard it's only recently that spies have been permitted to tell their loved ones what they do for a living."

"Because he lived in White Church Bay his entire life with the exception of the few years he was away at veterinary college."

"Good point. I imagine the government figures dogs make the best kind of spy, since they can't talk and give away sensitive information to the wrong people."

Harriet chuckled. "True. It's a shame Grandad didn't write a bit of the history behind the subject of each of his paintings. Visitors to the gallery would find stories like these fascinating."

"We could probably glean quite a few background stories from his journals and write them up. He's mentioned various paintings a few times in the journals I've read."

"That's not a bad idea. I could ask Mrs. Winslow to write the stories she remembers too. I know she regularly shares a few favorites with tourists, but not every visitor takes the tour."

Polly checked the time. "We better get going. I texted Van that we're heading to town for supper and suggested he meet us at the park. I figured we could get something to go. That way it'll be more private to talk, but we'd also have a good view of tourists coming and going and have a better chance of spotting our suspects."

"Good plan. Let me feed Maxwell and Charlie, and I'll be ready to leave. Will you invite Aunt Jinny?"

Her aunt turned down the invite, citing a fussy baby. An hour later, Harriet and Polly had long since finished the sausage rolls and cucumber salads they'd picked up from the Happy Cup Tearoom and Bakery, but there was still no sign of Van or their suspects.

"Did he acknowledge your text?" Harriet asked. "Maybe he didn't see us and went to Cobble Hill."

"Jinny would've called." Polly pulled out her phone and unlocked the screen. "No new messages. Wait—he replied back almost immediately, and I missed it."

"I hate when that happens. What did he say?"

Polly stood. "He's not coming. He got called away." She tossed the takeout containers into the nearby trash can. "What do you say we stroll the town? We could stop by Tales and Treasures. They sell toys as well as books, so our rucksack couple might've gone in there for gifts or souvenirs."

"I'm game." Harriet wasn't sure what to say to the couple if they found them. Hopefully, she and Polly could chat enough with them to learn where they were staying. If they spotted the guys in sunglasses, on the other hand, she'd prefer to not engage with them. Instead, they might try to follow them to see where they went.

All the shops were still adorned in bunting and proudly flying the Yorkshire flag with its white rose on a blue background. Tales and Treasures was a small corner shop with a ton of character, starting with the gorgeous, brightly colored bow windows on either side of the door. Polly introduced the young woman who greeted them as Susan, a classmate from her school days.

While Polly quizzed her friend on customers, describing the people they were searching for in detail, Harriet admired the toys displayed in the front window and chose a little wooden car to give Benji. As she made her way to the cash register, she spotted some hand-knitted animals and decided to switch out the car, which he was still too young to enjoy, for a zebra he could cuddle. She remembered hearing somewhere that high-contrast colors were easier for infants to see.

"I love these," Susan gushed as Harriet joined them at the checkout desk. "Who's it for?"

"Clive and Rowena Talbot's little boy. Do you know them?" Harriet slanted a sideways glance at Polly. She wasn't saying anything she shouldn't. Just seeing what Susan knew. After all, they'd learned things from Mr. Bellingham because he'd recognized Benji.

Susan wrapped the toy zebra. "Rowena comes in a lot. I met her husband for the first time when they came to the shop last week. He's gorgeous. If I were her, I'd be paranoid with all the traveling he does."

Harriet's eyes widened at the suggestion.

Susan immediately backpedaled. "Not that I'm saying he would stray. I don't know the man, but he seemed really nice. Although it was weird."

"What was weird?" Polly asked.

Susan's gaze drifted to a shelf of crib mobiles. "When they came in, Rowena said they came to buy a mobile for the baby, but her husband—Clive, did you say his name was?"

"That's it."

"Well, he started looking at the magazines then came over here and asked me if we had a copy of *Architecture Today*. I said if it's not on display, then we don't and apologized."

"Perhaps he's interested in renovating their home," Harriet suggested.

"No, that wasn't the weird part," Susan said. "He asked me to check the stock under the counter. That's where my boss keeps books and stuff people have ordered in special. He hadn't told me about anything like that, but I looked anyway, and sure enough, I found a copy of the magazine Clive wanted. There was no sticky note on it saying it was for him or anyone else, like there normally would be, so I sold it to him."

"That is a little weird," Polly agreed.

"Not only that," Susan added. "He hurried Rowena out before she got a chance to even look at the mobiles."

"Very odd. Thank you." Harriet paid for the stuffed zebra and headed out of the shop with Polly.

"Do you think there could've been a coded message in the magazine?" Polly asked. "I saw that in a movie once. Except the guy who picked up the magazine in the movie was an undercover operative, not a thief."

Harriet chuckled. "I'm pretty sure Clive was after reno ideas. Why would he swap clandestine messages with his criminal pals when he could pick up the phone and call or text them?"

"Good point. But he could still be a spy."

Harriet rolled her eyes. "Reading Grandad's journals has your imagination working overtime."

"Maybe, maybe not. Think about it. It could explain Clive's frequent trips, the scar, Rowena's blue mood, and why someone might kidnap her."

CHAPTER SIXTEEN

Harriet gaped at Polly, her mind whirling over the suggestion that Rowena's husband could be a spy. "That's crazy," she said a little too loudly. Remembering there could be listening ears around them, she lowered her voice to a whisper. "What could he possibly find to spy on in White Church Bay?"

"He travels all the time, remember?" Polly grabbed Harriet's arm. "Maybe he's an undercover operative, and he moved to our tiny out-of-the-way community to keep his family's identity a secret. But it didn't work."

"It wouldn't have been very smart of him to choose a tourist town like White Church Bay if he wanted to avoid being seen with his wife by the wrong people," Harriet reasoned, even as a part of her wondered if it could be true. For Benji's sake, she preferred that possibility to the one that his father was a criminal.

"I wonder if Mr. Bellingham has a key to the Talbots' place, since he's taking care of their cat. Come on." Polly started back up the hill. "We can tell him we need to pick up a few things for Benji, like more clothes. Jinny bought him a couple of new outfits, but she could use a couple more. While we're getting his things we can try to find the magazine Susan sold Clive at the same time. See if we can find a secret message in it."

Harriet jogged to keep up with Polly. "Seriously? You want to break into his house?"

"It's not breaking in if you have a key."

"I don't know if I agree with that," Harriet said.

But Polly kept walking.

Reaching the steps built into the sidewalk halfway up the hill, Harriet grabbed the handrail and stopped to catch her breath. "Think about it. Whatever or whoever Clive is, do you really think he'd leave a spare key to his house with the neighbor? He'd guard against the possibility of someone snooping and finding out something they shouldn't."

Polly pursed her lips. "Or he would leave a key with the neighbor because he would have hidden anything suspicious so well that anyone searching his place would conclude he was a nobody."

"Then what makes you think *we'll* find anything?" Harriet asked.

"Because we know about the magazine. We won't be idly snooping."

"Okay, you win." Harriet started climbing the stairs alongside Polly. "But do we know where the Talbots live?"

Polly grinned. "I know where the Bellinghams live. It was on their invoice. If Mr. Bellingham has a key, he'll probably let us into the Talbots' place."

Harriet scanned the people they passed but didn't spot the men in sunglasses from the other night at the Crow's Nest, or Mr. and Mrs. Rucksack. The street Polly led her to was strictly residences, so it wasn't clogged with tourists.

As luck would have it, Mr. Bellingham was outside his house deadheading flowers. When Polly explained their legitimate reason for wanting to be let into the Talbot house while remaining mum about their secondary goal, Harriet wondered if she should be worried by how adept her receptionist seemed to be at deflection.

"I suppose that'd be okay," the man said, and guilt stirred in Harriet's stomach.

Mr. Bellingham accompanied them inside—responsible on his part, but not ideal for them.

Harriet eyed every table and shelf on the way to the baby's room. "We should check the kitchen for more formula too," she said loud enough for Mr. Bellingham to hear from where he waited for them in the living room.

Polly whispered to Harriet, "I'll lead him into the kitchen, which will give you a better chance to check the other rooms more closely." She left Harriet to collecting outfits and diapers. Harriet heard her asking Mr. Bellingham if he would hold a chair for her to reach a high shelf in the kitchen.

Harriet hurried out of the baby's room and glanced in the remaining two bedrooms. One was the master bedroom, and the other was set up like a study. She quickly checked shelves and drawers then dashed to the living room. She didn't see magazines of any description anywhere, but she did notice ashes from what appeared to be the remains of a burned paper or papers on the fireplace grate.

Harriet scanned the mantel and the corners of the ceiling with the sudden uncomfortable thought that someone who communicated with people through secret messages in magazines would undoubtedly mount hidden cameras in his house to watch what people were up to when they were inside unsupervised.

Polly emerged from the kitchen with a rolled-up magazine and a tin of infant formula. "We'd better get going."

They rushed out, all smiles and cheery waves until they were out of Mr. Bellingham's sight. Then Harriet's feigned gusto gushed from her body, leaving her limp with trepidation. "You do realize that now Clive Talbot may have us on security footage snooping around his house, don't you?"

"Sure, but he won't report us if he doesn't want us to share our suspicions with the police, right?"

Maybe Harriet was tired, but Polly's logic actually made sense to her.

"Let's go to your place and see if we can figure out what was so important to Clive in this magazine," Polly suggested. "It might be the key to explaining Rowena's disappearance."

They hurried back to Cobble Hill.

"Let's go through it with Aunt Jinny," Harriet said. "She'll be eager for an update, and three heads are better than two when trying to solve a puzzle."

Aunt Jinny did not react well to learning of their snooping, but she was grateful for the fresh clothes and formula for Benji. And she knew a surprising number of ways ciphers were written and decoded. "Dominic enjoyed books and movies like that," she said, a wistful expression flitting across her face at the thought of her late husband. "It's amazing how many tidbits one picks up."

"Any ideas about what we should be looking for?" Harriet asked.

"It's possible we'll find an article with certain letters spelling out a message. Or he might have a code book at home that serves as a cipher key." Aunt Jinny explained additional methods of decoding as she leafed through the magazine. Then she dropped it on its narrow spine, and it flopped to one side. "I was checking whether it fell open to a specific page," she said. "The problem is that he doesn't seem to have opened this magazine at all. There are no coffee stains, dog-ears, pen marks—nothing."

"I did notice ashes on the fire grate, about the amount you'd expect from a sheet of paper," Harriet said.

"What if he ripped out the page he needed, then read and burned it?" Polly suggested.

Aunt Jinny thumbed through the magazine again, this time examining the page numbers. "Not a single page is missing."

"What about the last one before the back cover?" Polly said. "He could've carefully taken out that page without us missing a number."

Aunt Jinny retrieved her magnifying glass and examined the magazine's binding. "If he took a leaf out, he was meticulous about it. I can't see a shred of paper left along the spine."

Harriet picked up one of the magazines on Aunt Jinny's coffee table from the collection she read before putting them in her waiting room. An insert fluttered to the ground. "The magazine could have had a loose advertising insert in it, or even a regular piece of paper. Then after he read his message or whatever it was, he burned it."

Aunt Jinny frowned. "It's possible, I suppose. But not proof. I think we've let our imaginations get the better of us. What did Van have to say?"

"He never showed," Polly grumbled. "He claimed he'd been called out, but if you ask me, he's avoiding us. Maybe Clive's handlers have warned him off the whole thing."

Aunt Jinny chuckled. "Listen to us. This is White Church Bay in North Yorkshire. What on earth would spies be doing here?"

"They have to live somewhere," Polly said defensively.

"Will did mention that Clive seemed to be aware of a lot of things happening with world events that other people aren't," Harriet added, more inclined to side with Polly after seeing the small pile of ashes in the fire grate. She hoped she was wrong about the hidden cameras, or government agents might show up in the night to interrogate them.

"Well, I suggest we wait to hear what Van has to say about all this in the morning," Aunt Jinny said in a voice that brooked no argument. "If you present your spy theory to him and he's in the know, he'll give himself away. That lad couldn't lie to save his life."

Harriet thought of how readily he blushed the moment Polly talked to him and thought that Aunt Jinny was probably right.

By the time Harriet returned from her morning farm calls on Tuesday, Van was already there and Polly was already laying into him.

"What was so important yesterday that you couldn't spare us twenty minutes of your time?" Polly griped. "Do you know that Clive Talbot has a gunshot wound on his arm?"

"We don't know that it's a gunshot wound," Harriet reminded her.

"What's that got to do with Rowena's disappearance and your stolen painting?" Van countered. "No one said anything about shots being fired."

Clearly taken aback by his response, Polly opened her mouth, but no words came out.

"We thought it might be further proof that he's involved in some criminal enterprise," Harriet explained. Perhaps they should wait to float the spy theory until they had more evidence.

"I haven't been ignoring the case," Van told them. "Yesterday, they picked up Rowena's cell phone signal. And last night, York police raided the location it was last pinpointed."

Harriet straightened, triumph surging through her veins. "They found her?"

Van's jaw tightened. "We found her phone. It was in the back seat of a tourist's car outside a hotel. York police are following up."

"Have they made an arrest?"

Van shook his head. "The couple who rented the car did drive to Cobble Hill Farm to visit the gallery the day of the burglary. After that, they continued their tour of Yorkshire by spending the weekend hiking and camping out, which explains why we weren't able to pick up the cell phone signal until yesterday. They were nowhere near here."

"Are they our rucksack couple?" Polly asked.

"They can't be," Harriet said. "Will and I saw them Saturday afternoon out near the Staveley farm."

"They could've lied to the police about where they went," Polly argued. "Are the police checking the car's GPS history to verify? And even if they did go where they claim, it doesn't mean they didn't get rid of Rowena up there or fence the painting to some lowlife along the way."

"They aren't your kidnappers or thieves," Van insisted.

"How can you be sure?" Harriet asked.

"Detectives interrogate enough suspects and witnesses to know when they're being lied to."

That seemed like flimsy reasoning to Harriet. "Then how did Rowena's phone end up in their car?"

"When they were asked if they left their car unlocked, they said no but recalled that a dark-haired man approached them when they were getting into their car. They said he was very friendly—asked where they were from and where they were going then made a couple of suggestions of must-see sights."

Harriet gritted her teeth. Leave it to a slimy thief to use a couple of innocent tourists to throw the scent off himself.

"They'd opened all the doors to clear the heat from the car and were distracted pulling their picnic lunch from the boot while they were chatting with him. It would've been easy for him to slip the phone under the front seat unnoticed."

A guy described as friendly didn't sound like the ones who had been watching her and Polly. Then again, a criminal no doubt learned to be a good actor to get what he wanted, if brute force wouldn't do it. Remembering the description Polly's friend had given of the guy who'd asked after Clive at the coast guard station, Harriet asked, "Did they describe him? Was he tall with a faint scar on his chin by any chance?"

Van's jaw muscle flexed. "I really shouldn't be sharing information from an ongoing investigation."

"We're the ones who found Rowena's baby and alerted you that she was missing," Harriet retorted, feeling her temper fray.

"About that. I left Dr. Garrett a voice mail last night. Did she tell you?"

"Tell us what?"

"The baby's father is aware of the situation and wants Benji to remain in her care until Rowena is found."

All Harriet could do was gape.

Polly found her voice first. "You've actually talked to him? Seen him?"

"I haven't. DI McCormick relayed the message to me to give to Dr. Garrett so she'd stop leaving messages on Mr. Talbot's phone. She called his house phone too. And we wouldn't want the wrong person picking up that message."

"And come after Benji, you mean?" Harriet shuddered at the prospect.

Van fell silent again.

"We have a right to know if someone might come after Benji," Harriet insisted.

"We don't know, do we?" Van said at last. "That's why the fewer people who know he's here, the better. The safer you'll all be."

"Is that why Clive hasn't come to see Benji?" Polly asked. "Because he doesn't want to be seen here?"

"That'd be my guess."

"Who's Detective Ascot?" Harriet asked. "With the York Regional Crime Squad."

Van cocked his head. "I don't know any Detective Ascot. Why?"

"How can you not know him? He's working Rowena's disappearance."

Van's eyes narrowed. "What makes you say that? Did this fellow talk to you?"

"No. He questioned the Talbots' neighbor, Mr. Bellingham, who showed us the detective's card. It said he was from the York Regional Crime Squad." Harriet searched Van's gaze, trying to read his reaction to the news. "Have they taken you off the case?"

"Listen, I go where I'm told." His tone was defensive.

"All the better reason to find out if Detective Ascot exists," Polly said. "Because if he doesn't and someone's impersonating a detective, clearly there's more going on here than a simple theft and a rash decision to kidnap a witness. You could be the one to crack it wide open. Did your boss tell you this case involved national security?"

Van burst out laughing. "Hardly. What kind of criminal do you think Clive is?"

"*Is* he a criminal?" Harriet demanded.

"I already told you Sunday—not that we know of."

"A spy then?" Polly asked. There went Harriet's idea to keep that theory between them.

The amusement in Van's eyes vanished. "I doubt it. Where do you two come up with these notions? Are you sleeping enough?"

Harriet exchanged a glance with Polly, not eager to divulge that they'd searched the Talbot house under false pretenses. "When things don't make sense, sometimes you have to think outside the box."

"It's also a mistake to operate on those theories without evidence."

Harriet planted her hands on her hips. "Is there evidence we don't know about, Detective Constable?"

"I need to go." Van rose abruptly. "I'll let you know if we get any leads on the whereabouts of your grandfather's painting."

"What about on Rowena's whereabouts?" Polly needled.

"Best you don't concern yourself with that." Van let himself out before they could utter a syllable of protest.

"See?" Polly blurted. "He knows a whole lot more than he's saying."

"I'm not sure he does. His ignorance of Detective Ascot seemed genuine."

"If the man is even a detective," Polly said.

"Yeah. I'm sure Van will check on that."

Polly crossed her arms over her chest. "If you ask me, he should be taking a closer look at Rowena's husband. What kind of man doesn't fly home the moment he hears his wife's disappeared and his son is in foster care?"

The same thought had been rattling around Harriet's brain. A man who knows what's really going on and is trying to contain it, maybe. But did that make him a criminal? Or some kind of puppet, with someone else pulling his strings?

Whatever the scenario, it was clear to Harriet that Clive Talbot had secrets.

CHAPTER SEVENTEEN

"Harriet? Barry Tweedy here."

"Yes, hello, Barry." Harriet managed not to sigh at the sound of her colleague's voice on the other end of the phone. She liked the good doctor, and as much as she hoped he had some news for her, she'd been looking forward to a quiet tea break after an altercation with an otherwise mild-mannered Persian cat while trimming his claws.

Polly shot Harriet a sympathetic glance from the other side of the dining room table.

"Listen," Barry continued, "I've been thinking about those sick cows and have come up with a possibility."

Harriet instantly straightened and set down her tea. "What's that?"

"Louping Ill virus. Are the cattle grazing the moors with sheep?"

"I don't think so. There are sheep in fields in the area, so perhaps they intermix. I'm not sure."

"Oh." The optimism drained from his voice. "How old is the first calf that got sick?"

"Ten or twelve weeks, I believe."

"So it might not have been dipped for ticks yet. Did you check for ticks on him?"

Her heart thudded in her chest. "Not specifically, no." Why hadn't she thought to check for ticks? They carried any number of diseases. "I did check the hide over thoroughly for wounds and didn't encounter any ticks."

"I know how thorough you are, but ticks can be particularly difficult to spot."

As he spoke, Harriet looked up the disease on her phone. When he paused, she read off the symptoms, which were similar to what she'd encountered in Staveley's cows.

"You're familiar with it?" Barry asked.

"No, I found this online. I did take tissue samples yesterday to examine under a microscope, but I don't have an electron microscope, so I wouldn't expect to see this virus."

"You haven't heard back from the lab?" he asked sympathetically.

"If I'm lucky, I might by tomorrow. The samples would have been delivered close to closing time on Saturday."

"With lab technicians in and out on their summer holidays, results seem to be taking longer than usual."

Harriet thanked him for calling and made a mental note to ask Mr. Staveley about his tick-prevention routine though the symptoms of this particular virus weren't exactly what she was seeing in the sick cows. Since Gilbert Vail's call on Sunday, there'd been no new reports of cows with symptoms, so that was something. Maybe bringing them off the moors had done some good.

At the jingle of the bell over the door, Polly hurried out to reception. A moment later, she called down the hall to where Harriet was still finishing her tea. "Mrs. Stoddelmeier is here to pick up Naughty. I'll fetch him from the kennel."

Naughty was a young mixed-breed dog that was proving to be a handful for the young Stoddelmeier family, who had left him with Harriet for observation to see if she had any advice to help calm him. Having confirmed his energy levels were normal for his age, Harriet had emailed them a report stating he would benefit from two long walks a day and lots of games of fetch or tag in the garden with the children. *A tired dog is a good dog.*

Harriet went out to ask Mrs. Stoddelmeier if they'd enjoyed their quiet time with the dog away, but the woman must have followed Polly to the kennel.

When Polly returned after seeing Mrs. Stoddelmeier off, she showed Harriet a massive brown egg. "Look what I almost stepped on in the barn. What do you suppose laid this? A wild pheasant?"

"No. Their eggs are a pale olive green." Harriet took the egg to examine more closely. "They can be brown, but they're smaller than hen eggs. The egg isn't warm, so whatever laid it doesn't seem interested in it hatching. Do you have wild turkeys in Yorkshire?"

"Not to my knowledge. The closest we have is the red grouse."

"But their eggs are pale with dark brown blotches. Maybe one of Doreen's hens went on a walk."

Polly chuckled. "I'll give her a call and suggest she do a head count. Meanwhile, if you want to eat it, I'd suggest cracking it in a bowl first to make sure it hasn't gone bad."

Harriet glanced at her watch. "I am hungry. I wouldn't mind scrambling some eggs before the next appointment. Did you want some?"

Polly declined. Harriet took the egg to the kitchen to scramble with a couple more, a splash of milk, and a dash of Worcestershire sauce. She'd taken to adding the British invention to many of her dishes since moving to the UK, loving the extra tang it gave to foods. She cracked the gift egg first, and to her surprise, two yolks came out, reminding her of Alfie's story about Rosie. Harriet cracked one from his dozen next, another double-yolker of identical size and color to the first.

Harriet quickly cooked the eggs then topped them with a dollop of brown sauce, which she'd also grown astoundingly fond of.

Polly stuck her head through the doorway. "Your next appointment is here."

"Be right there. Thanks. Did you talk to Allen when you called the clients we had in on Friday? I think this egg might have been a gift from his Rosie."

"Two yolks?"

"Yes."

Polly grinned. "He was out when I called. I explained the situation to his mother, and she said she'd ask him."

"We should really talk to him. Maybe he got here early and took Rosie to the barn to see the animals. If he was there when those guys Doreen saw were around, he might have gotten a better look at them."

"Do you want me to call and ask him to stop by?"

"It might be better if we stop by his place later. Since the police don't seem worried about Benji staying here, I hope that means they don't expect any more trouble on our doorstep, but I'm not sure we can count on it. In fact, we might be smart to ask the police to drive by regularly if they aren't already."

"Jinny didn't tell you?"

"Tell me what?"

"After you left Saturday, the police sent over a guy to mount motion-triggered security cameras on the drive and around the houses that they can monitor remotely for as long as Benji stays at the farm."

Harriet shuddered. "That sounds as if they think the kidnapper will come back."

"I thought the same."

"Then why are they leaving Benji here? Are they using him as bait?" Anger sharpened Harriet's tone. Not that she wanted to see the baby shuffled off to yet another stranger's home, but his safety was more important than what she wanted.

"I think they wanted to put you and Jinny at ease."

Harriet willed her stampeding pulse to slow. If Aunt Jinny was comfortable with the situation, then she should be too. Not to mention grateful for the extra measure of security.

When Harriet joined Polly at the reception desk following their last appointment of the afternoon, Polly informed her that Mr. Williams had called to ask for Harriet to assess his new bull.

Harriet racked her brain but couldn't conjure an image of the man. "Have I been to the Williams farm before?"

"No, but your grandad always said it was a pleasant drive, though it's just shy of an hour each way and hilly. When would you like me to schedule the visit?"

"Maybe I better go now." Although there was no urgency, being such a long drive away from the clinic meant that just getting there and back would consume a lot of time. If an emergency arose, Polly would have to move their scheduled appointments. "We can save talking to Allen for the morning."

"Sounds good. I'll call Mr. Williams to let him know."

As Harriet battled the Beast's temperamental clutch and gears while negotiating the roller-coaster terrain between Cobble Hill and the Williams farm, her thoughts strayed to her grandfather and the many times he must have traveled this very route. After a busy day, it was lovely to have the mental and physical break of a quiet country drive.

The sun was still high enough to not be in her eyes. It was low enough, however, that the hills, or fells as they called them in the moorlands, cast long shadows over the valleys below. The hills were dotted with sheep and, on occasion, their bleating rivaled the rumble of her motor.

She spotted the sign for the Williams farm and turned down the drive. The house, made of Yorkshire stone, was connected to the garage, which was connected to the barn. The arrangement formed a sort of courtyard where a couple of tractors and other equipment sat.

Mr. Williams emerged from the courtyard, extending his hand. "You must be the vet. My name's Grady."

Harriet returned his greeting, taking in his fledgling operation with a visual sweep of the barns and surrounding pasture. A bull would represent a significant investment for a farm this size, which explained why he was willing to pay for her opinion about him.

Grady led her to where the new bull awaited her examination. "Isn't he grand?"

Harriet nodded. "He's a beauty." Half an hour later, following a thorough examination and testing, she stood by the declaration.

With a grin that stretched from ear to ear, Grady whipped off his hat and slapped it against his thigh. "That's wonderful. Good to know he was worth the pretty penny I spent on him."

Harriet mirrored the joy on his face with a grin of her own. It reminded her of the story of Mr. Henderson's pride in the bull in Grandad's painting. The thought of the missing painting left her itching to do more to try to find it.

But what?

CHAPTER EIGHTEEN

The blare of her phone jolted Harriet awake Wednesday morning, but the light filtering past the bedroom curtains was moonlight, not dawn. She blindly patted her bedside table in search of her phone.

Finally finding it, Harriet answered the call. "Cobble Hill Veterinary."

"Harriet, it's me. Can you come over and stay with Benji? I have an emergency."

Harriet sprang from her bed, fully awake. "I'll be right there." She grabbed the clothes she'd set out for the next morning and hurried downstairs with them tucked under her arm.

Maxwell whined from his bed in the corner.

"It's okay, boy. Go back to sleep." Slipping out the door, Harriet jogged to Aunt Jinny's.

A flicker in the trees caught her eye, but she couldn't make out what was there. Was that where the police had mounted one of their cams? She hugged her clothes to her chest, rethinking the wisdom of flying out of the house in her night clothes. If they were really watching the cameras 24-7, she hoped they realized it was her dashing across the yard and didn't send out the cavalry.

Aunt Jinny met her at the door, her black bag in hand. "Benji's asleep in the guest room. He shouldn't need to be fed again until six. There's another bottle already made up in the fridge. If—"

"Don't worry. We'll be fine."

With a nod, Aunt Jinny dashed into the night. Harriet went into the guest room and fixed the covers on the sleeping infant, resisting the urge to pick him up for a cuddle, then got into the nearby bed to try to catch more sleep herself.

When she woke, light streamed into the room, and it took her a moment to remember where she was. She padded over to check on Benji.

The crib was empty.

Her heart flew into her throat, and she raced to Aunt Jinny's bedroom. Finding it empty, she pounded down the stairs. "Please tell me you're here, Aunt Jinny!"

Aunt Jinny stepped out of the kitchen with Benji safely cradled in her arms as Harriet skidded around the corner.

Harriet's breath left in a whoosh. "You scared me half to death."

Aunt Jinny chuckled. "Sorry. He started to fuss when I got home, so I thought I'd take care of the feeding and let you sleep."

"I'll do that." Harriet reached for the bottle. "You must be exhausted."

"I'm fine. Adrenaline is still doing its thing." Aunt Jinny passed Benji into Harriet's arms and handed her the bottle. "But I'd love a long shower."

"What was the emergency?"

Aunt Jinny beamed. "A seven-pound, chubby-cheeked baby girl with the fullest head of dark hair I've ever seen on a newborn.

Mother and baby are both doing great. I arrived in time to catch the wee babe as she arrived."

Harriet chuckled, smiling down at the baby in her arms. "It's a great feeling, isn't it? Of course, I've only had the privilege of bringing babies of the four-footed variety into the world." She tipped the bottle to Benji's lips, and exhilaration filled her when he accepted it on her first attempt.

"It is wonderful. I've delivered so many, but the thrill of it never gets old."

Harriet glanced at the newspaper lying open on the kitchen table and gasped. "I forgot to cancel the ad for the unveiling of Grandad's painting this weekend. Is that this week's paper?"

"It is. Polly or Mrs. Winslow must have taken care of canceling the ad. I didn't see it in there," Aunt Jinny said.

Wincing at the thought of what the reporter, Fraser Kemp, might have written about the burglary, Harriet thumbed through the paper. "Did they run an article on the gallery?"

"No, there's nothing in the paper about the gallery. Are you sure that reporter you spoke to was one from our local paper?"

Harriet jolted at the question. "I don't think I asked. I assumed. He seemed to know Grandad very well."

"Maybe that's why he sat on his burglary scoop—out of deference for an old friend." Aunt Jinny headed off to shower, and Harriet sat at the kitchen table to continue feeding Benji.

When he finished his bottle, she carefully lifted him to her shoulder to burp him as she scanned the newspaper for other articles with Fraser's byline. But there weren't any. An uneasy sensation bloomed in Harriet's gut. She flipped back to the second page and read the names in the small box in the bottom corner that listed the publisher, editor, and numerous reporters, but again, Fraser's name wasn't among them. Maybe he used a nom de plume. But wouldn't that have been the name he would have given her if that was the case?

She pulled out her phone and searched for the paper's website. It had a long list of contributors, but Fraser Kemp wasn't among them. Next, she did a search on his name. She hit on a page that identified him as a freelance reporter from North Yorkshire. Aside from that, his profile was astonishingly thin, almost as if…

As if it had been manufactured in a hurry.

She shook her head. For what purpose? He'd arranged the appointment with Mrs. Winslow the day before he'd arrived. Maybe not before the painting was stolen and Rowena went missing, but more than half a day before they reported anything to the police.

Mrs. Winslow said the reporter had been inspired to write an article because of Callum's blog. Maybe what he'd really been inspired to do was get a behind-the-scenes look at the gallery's holdings and security to plan a heist. But someone else beat him to it.

Benji squawked.

Harriet jerked her attention back to the infant. "I'm sorry, sweetie. I'm letting my imagination get the better of me these days. The nice reporter was probably hoping to sell his article to a bigger paper. After all, he knew my grandfather and would be able to give the article a more personal touch." Harriet tickled the baby's tummy, and he gave her a heart-melting smile. "You really are adorable."

He caught her finger and held on tight.

"You would've liked my grandfather," she continued, since he seemed to like to listen to her voice. "Like the reporter said, everyone was a friend to him." She tilted her head at the memory. She'd asked Fraser if he was Grandad's friend, but he hadn't exactly answered the question. She reflected on what else he'd said about her grand-father and about his affection for her. They were personal things, but not anything a good reporter couldn't have picked up by talking to anyone who knew Doc Bailey. Not once did Fraser say that he and Grandad had actually spoken.

Benji started to fuss.

Harriet rolled the stress from her shoulders and pasted on a smile. "Never mind me. I'm being silly. I'm sure we have nothing to worry about from the likes of Fraser Kemp."

She stood and strolled around the house to give him a change of scenery. "I'll tell you what. I'll get dressed, and we can walk around out-side. I know Charlie would like to see you again." She set Benji in the crib while she changed then scooped him up once more and called to her aunt through the bathroom door that they were heading outside.

The instant she stepped out, Charlie sprang up and twined around her legs. "Have you been playing guard cat out here all night?" She sat on the step so the cat could see Benji, and Charlie purred loudly. Harriet scratched the cat's neck. "You're going to miss our little visitor when he goes home, aren't you?" Her heart kicked at the idea. "Me too." She pressed a kiss to the top of Benji's head, inhaling his sweet baby scent even as she tamped down a swell of longing. The scripture that had buoyed her flagging optimism after Dustin broke off their engagement returned to her thoughts—*I know the plans I have for you.*

She pushed to her feet and ambled around the back of the cot-tage to the path along the cliff's edge with Charlie trotting alongside.

She might not be married and welcoming a baby of her own. But life was good.

The sun had just crested the hill and was burning off the morning mist. Gratitude filled her heart for her grandfather's generosity, which had paved the way for her to come here. *I know you don't promise us an easy life, Lord, but please don't let our efforts here be for nothing.*

Taking a few moments to look out over the sea, she registered the head of foam on the turbulent water, the red tinge in the sky. "We might be in for a stormy day," she said aloud to Benji and Charlie. They headed back, reaching the parking area as Polly pulled in.

"You're early," Harriet called to her.

"You said you were going to speak to Allen this morning before the clinic opens, so I thought I'd come along."

Harriet glanced at her watch. "Yes, we should do that now." She asked Polly to take care of attaching Maxwell's wheels and letting him out while she took Benji to Aunt Jinny.

"You haven't had breakfast yet," Aunt Jinny protested when Harriet told her she and Polly were leaving. "Sit down. I fried us eggs. It'll take Polly a few minutes to tend to the dog anyway."

Harriet's stomach grumbled, so she polished off a couple of eggs with fried tomatoes on a slice of toast before Polly tapped on the door, then took tea to go in a thermal cup. "We want to catch Allen at home," she explained to Aunt Jinny, "before he heads to wherever it is young boys get off to on their summer breaks."

"We found evidence he might have hung out around the barn Friday afternoon," Polly added, "and we want to find out if he saw the blokes in sunglasses that Doreen noticed, or if he saw anyone else acting suspicious."

"Don't scare the poor boy by mentioning Rowena going missing, will you? We don't know for sure she was kidnapped." Aunt Jinny's voice cracked. Neither scenario boded well for Rowena, considering if she wasn't kidnapped, she was likely a thief who'd abandoned her child for a few thousand pounds.

"We won't. But kids are resilient," Harriet said, glancing at Benji. "We'll see you later."

Allen's family farm was a few miles west of Cobble Hill. His father raised sheep mostly but also had a few head of cattle, a flock of chickens, and was even fattening a pig for a winter's supply of bacon and sausages. When her grandfather was a boy, such a self-sufficient variety of animals was typical of most small holdings in the area, but not so much anymore.

As Harriet waited for a trail of goslings to finish following their mother across the driveway in front of her truck, Allen's father came around a nearby barn and eyed her suspiciously. The moment she parked, he jutted his chin and demanded in a harsh voice, "What are you doing here? I didn't call for the vet. There's nothing wrong with my cows, so don't you be telling me mine need to be quarantined."

Harriet bristled. Word of the quarantine she'd imposed on the Staveleys' cows had obviously made the rounds of the farming community. She grimaced at Polly, whose job also hung in the balance if Harriet's decision to quarantine the cattle kept other farmers in the area from availing themselves of her services. Taking a fortifying breath, she climbed out of the truck. "I'm not here about your cattle, Mr. Aimes. I was hoping to speak to Allen."

The tension in the man's stance eased, and a flicker of a smile twitched the corner of his lips. "That was a right fine job you did on his Rosie's leg. She's a good bird."

Harriet grinned. "She is indeed."

The man bellowed for his son, who came racing from behind the barn. "The vet needs to talk to you."

The eagerness washed from Allen's face. He toed at the gravel as his dad bade them good day and then returned to the barn. The instant his dad was out of earshot, he blurted, "Mum told me you called. She was going to call you back as soon as you opened. I'm real sorry, Miss Harriet." His voice sounded pitiful, and Harriet had to wonder what exactly his mom had said.

"There's nothing for you to worry about, Allen," Harriet said gently. "We were hoping you might have seen something that would help us know who took the painting. We found one of Rosie's eggs in the barn. At least we think it was one of hers, since it had two yolks. We thought you might have hung around the farm for a while on Friday morning."

He gulped visibly, and she hastened to add, "Which is absolutely fine. But it's not a good idea to take Rosie into the barn, since you never know what illness she might catch from an animal we're nursing. Or what she might be carrying that could harm the other animals."

"It's my fault," he insisted. "I dared him."

"Dared who?"

"Alfie. He was showing me the animals he feeds and waters for you, and then we saw those men pulling the ivy off the other building, and Alfie told me you kept paintings inside. He said that was why all those tourists were lining up. He snuck me in the back door, but he said it was all right, that you wouldn't mind."

"I honestly don't," she said softly, her hopes surging. "Did you see someone sneak off with the painting and not want to say anything because it would mean admitting you snuck in yourself?"

He shook his head, his eyes bright. "We didn't know you thought you got robbed. No one told us."

Harriet exchanged a baffled glance with Polly. "Is that why you didn't say anything sooner? Because you didn't know the significance of what you saw?"

His gaze snapped to hers, his furrowed brow suggesting they were talking about two different things. "We didn't see anything."

His earlier exclamation—*we didn't know you thought you got robbed*—sank in. "Are you saying no one stole the painting?"

"Please don't give Alfie the boot. He needs the job for the cat's medicine. His dad can't afford it, and the cat means everything to his sister." Allen scarcely paused for breath. "He said he and you joke around all the time. That you're a good sort. We thought you'd see it. We didn't know you called the police. Alfie never saw them there." Allen lifted his gaze from the ground for an instant to nod toward Polly. "Except for that nice DC who's sweet on her."

Before Polly could splutter her usual protest, Harriet caught Allen by the shoulders, scarcely resisting the impulse to shake the rest of the story out of him. She knelt in front of him, forcing him to meet her gaze. "You're saying Alfie moved the painting we thought was stolen?"

"He did, but it's my fault. I dared him. I don't know what made me do it. You've been so kind about Rosie."

"Where did he put the painting?" Polly interjected in the firm voice she used when silencing a kennel full of barking dogs.

Allen lifted his chin as a tear streaked down his dusty cheek. "It's in the children's room at the back of the art gallery. I'm sure he figured you'd find it right away once you realized it was moved and that you'd know it was him who moved it."

Harriet surged to her feet and planted a kiss on the top of his head. "That's the best news I've heard in days." She injected a bit of sternness into her voice. "But don't let me catch you two doing anything so foolhardy again, okay? And of course he can keep his job. He's very good at it and a big help. Thank you for telling me the truth."

Wonder swept over his face, as if he'd clearly been expecting her to be angry.

Harriet and Polly raced back to Cobble Hill Farm. But it was still well before opening time, so Harriet had to fumble through her keys to find the one that unlocked the gallery door. The instant she had it open, Polly raced inside ahead of her, veering toward the small room set aside for youngsters. They both stepped inside and, slowly turning, assessed the room. Art created by dozens of children hung on the walls.

"It's not here," Polly said.

"It has to be." So much artwork had been tacked to the wall that more recent contributions overlapped older ones. Suddenly Harriet noticed that one of the larger pieces stood out from the wall. Her hopes rose, and she yanked the piece down and squealed with delight. She lifted her grandfather's framed painting from the wall. "Can you believe it was here all along? Allen and Alfie hid it well."

Harriet triumphantly carried the painting back to the easel in the storage room. "I guess we'll be able to have our grand unveiling this weekend after all."

Polly bit her lip.

"What is it?"

"I was thinking we need to tell Van the painting has been here all along. But you know what this means?"

Harriet draped the tarp over the painting, her mind scrambling to make sense. "What?"

"If Rowena's disappearance wasn't connected to an art heist, where is she?"

CHAPTER NINETEEN

Thanks to a full morning of back-to-back appointments, Harriet didn't have time to contemplate an explanation for Rowena's disappearance. She supposed their theory about it being connected to Clive's career, whether it be criminal or secretive, still sort of fit. Unfortunately, so did their initial fear that Rowena had wandered off for a momentary respite and been unable to return for some reason Harriet hated to entertain.

Apparently preoccupied with similar thoughts, Polly said, "I still think Rowena was kidnapped." She helped Harriet collect three kittens from the recovery room to return to their owner. "Mrs. Danby saw those two men in sunglasses 'escorting' a woman, remember? She assumed the woman was ill, but maybe she deliberately let her body go limp to make it more difficult to be carried off."

"Why not yell for help then?"

"Maybe they drugged her. Or threatened Benji."

They put the discussion on hold as Harriet gave the pet owner instructions on kitten care then hurried to the back to collect a black lab when his owner arrived. Once the last animal was out the door and the sign turned over to Closed, Harriet sank into a waiting room chair. "What did Van say about our news? Has Rowena's husband gotten a ransom call?"

"Van said now that there's no robbery to solve, he's no longer being kept in the loop."

"What?"

Polly slapped a patient's file closed. "Apparently, Detective Ascot handles missing persons for Yorkshire."

"Ascot?" Harriet stiffened. "The guy who spoke to Rowena's neighbor?"

"That's the one."

"Then why hasn't this detective questioned us?"

Polly shut down the computer. "Your guess is as good as mine. Maybe he figures that Van got all the information there was to get out of us."

"Or they have leads we know nothing about," Harriet added optimistically.

Polly retrieved her purse and hitched it over her shoulder. "I have an idea where we might find some leads of our own on Clive."

"Where's that?"

"At the annual interservice tug-of-war competition tonight in Whitby. The lifeboat volunteers will be there, as well as teams from the coast guard, police, firefighters, and probably paramedics. Everyone who might know something will all be in one place."

"I'm game. But how are we going to ply them for information without mentioning Rowena? I assume the police still want her disappearance kept quiet."

Polly's eyes twinkled. "Sure, but they didn't say anything about Clive. And besides the competitions, there'll be sales stalls and a raffle and a barbecue. Lots of fun stuff. When people are in a good mood, they usually get more talkative."

Harriet mulled it over then said, "I don't imagine it can do any harm."

"Great. Let me go home and freshen up, and then I'll come back for you."

The park was packed with people by the time they arrived, making it challenging to get close to HM Coastguard and RNLI personnel, never mind chat them up for information.

Alfie and his sister appeared beside Harriet and Polly as they watched the tug-of-war competition. "I didn't know you were coming tonight. My uncle is on the lifeboat team." Alfie pointed to a big-boned man anchoring the rope for the RNLI side. "I thought about greasing the rope, but I wasn't sure which side he'd be on."

Normally Harriet would have chuckled, but after all the trouble his mischief in the art gallery had caused, she wasn't in a laughing mood.

Polly laid into him. "Do you have any idea the stress your mischief has caused us? We thought that painting you *relocated* was stolen. The police took a report and dusted for fingerprints. They've wasted hours of time and who knows how much money trying to find that painting."

Alfie's eyes went round, and his face suddenly seemed a little green. "I'm sorry. I had no idea it would cause that much trouble. I thought the doc would see it right away and know I'd done it."

"You should be sorry," Polly scolded. "Your silly prank might have gotten a woman kidnapped."

"Shh," Harriet hissed as Alfie's jaw dropped and his sister's face paled.

"What are you talking about?" Alfie asked.

Harriet flashed Polly a glare. So much for keeping Rowena's disappearance under wraps.

"What's going on?" Alfie pressed.

Drawing in a lungful of air, Harriet glanced around. Everyone seemed preoccupied with watching the competition, so she drew Alfie and his sister aside to explain enough to make sure he didn't go around talking about what Polly said.

"I saw something," he exclaimed after hearing that a woman had disappeared from outside the gallery on Friday. "I saw a couple of shifty-looking blokes with a woman on Friday."

"Can you describe them?" Polly demanded.

Alfie's nose scrunched. "They both had dark hair. One was kind of skinny and wore jeans and a T-shirt. I remember the short sleeves because he had really hairy arms. The other guy was tall and had on a jacket with black jeans. I thought he must be sweating like crazy, it was so hot."

Impressed by the amount of detail he remembered, Harriet asked if he'd noticed any scars or if they wore sunglasses.

Alfie's voice perked up enthusiastically. "Shiny aviator glasses." He scratched the side of his head. "Come to think of it, the tall bloke in the jacket might've had a scar on his jaw."

Polly jabbed Harriet with her elbow then surreptitiously pointed to their left at the two men in sunglasses they'd seen at the Crow's Nest on Saturday night.

Harriet chewed on the bottom corner of her lip. How could they check out the guys without drawing attention to themselves?

Once again, Polly took the bull by the horns. "Don't make it obvious that you're looking," she whispered to Alfie, "but there's a couple of guys in sunglasses over there. Are those the same blokes you saw?"

Alfie shifted his gaze in the direction Polly indicated. "That's not them. There was at least a foot difference in height between the two blokes I saw. And the little guy I saw was smaller than both of those two. I'm really sorry. Can I go find my parents?"

Harriet nodded. When he turned away, she exchanged a glance with Polly. "They must be a different pair than the men we've been seeing."

Polly agreed. "Which means that these two don't have anything to do with Rowena."

Harriet studied the men in sunglasses from beneath her lashes. "But those two are definitely the ones we've seen before."

"And they seem more intent on scanning the crowds than watching the competition," Polly added.

Harriet gasped. "Did you see that?"

"What?"

"I thought I saw a gun in a shoulder holster under the tall one's windbreaker."

Polly grabbed her arm. "Let's get out of here."

CHAPTER TWENTY

T he next day, Harriet still hadn't shaken the panic sparked by the gun she thought she saw. During the drive back to Cobble Hill, she'd called Van to alert him and give him Alfie's more detailed description of Rowena's likely kidnappers. He'd taken the details to pass on to Detective Ascot. But his dismissive response to her concern about the men in sunglasses they'd just seen irked her.

Not to mention his strongly worded admonishment to stay away from the coast guard station and leave the detective work to Ascot's team.

She felt as if she'd been operating on autopilot most of the day. Thankfully, none of her cases so far had been too challenging. She had just finished sterilizing an exam room between patients when Polly announced the lab results from Mr. Staveley's cows were in.

Harriet dashed to the desk to scan the open email attachment on Polly's computer screen. "I was right. Lead poisoning. Which means the protocol I put the herd on may have spared them." Harriet did a little jig on her way to the supply room, where she sifted through the new boxes of pharmaceutical supplies that had come in.

Polly printed off the report and then followed Harriet to the supply room. "What's next?"

"We'll continue to monitor the herd—I mean fold." Finding the medications she was after, she added them to her bag. "And I'll do another inspection of the field."

"So we still have no idea where the cows came into contact with the lead?" Polly asked.

"No, and in light of how many cows have developed symptoms, I can't see it being something as simple as a dumped truck battery. The river water needs to be tested." Harriet grimaced. "It must be coming from an old mine or manufacturing plant. Would you like to join me for another scouting hike?"

"I can't tonight. I have a date."

"That's okay." Harriet opened her contact list on her phone. "I'll see if Will wants to join me."

"We could put the word out to the Ramblers Association. Ask them to be on the lookout for any obvious contamination."

"Good idea. Could you do that for me?"

"Sure."

An hour later, Harriet and Will set out on their second hike together in less than a week.

"I was thinking," Will said, "that instead of hunting every which way for a source of contamination, we should follow the cattle tracks to see where the animals have actually been."

"You're right. Let's do that." Harriet scanned the hillsides. "Hopefully, we can still find the tracks, considering the grass has had a few days to grow without being trampled on."

They trekked about the pastures for nearly two hours, covering all the high fields running from Goose Beck Farm, behind the old Henderson place, and right up to Gilbert Vail's farm, which she supposed now included Henderson's property, although she couldn't understand why Gilbert had let it go to ruin after all his finagling to own it in the first place. In almost a straight line as the crow flies, they spotted areas every hundred feet or so where the cows must have congregated to lie down in the field, because large areas were trampled rather than a narrow footpath.

After examining the third such area, Harriet toed the dirt. "We've got to be missing something. This has to be where they spent most of their time, but I don't see anything toxic anywhere. Do you?"

"Nope." Will squinted from where they stood to the similar spots they'd already been. "It's strange how they all seem to be in a row. Although maybe that's not unusual. I've never really paid attention to where the animals sleep on the moors."

Harriet's phone rang.

"You've got to get over to the Danby farm," Polly exclaimed. "There's been an accident, and the coast guard is involved in the rescue."

Harriet's pulse rioted. "Is one of the Danbys hurt?"

"No. The dog of some rambler on the cliffside trail went over the edge, and the owner got himself in a precarious spot trying to save the dog, which managed to scramble up all on its own."

Harriet frowned. "So the dog's okay?"

"Yes, but you still have to go. The *coast guard* is there. And not my friend's station. Clive's station. After they've rescued the man, I was thinking we could ask them about Clive."

"But Van—"

"Van said we weren't to go to the station. He didn't say anything about not talking to the guys that come to us."

"You were a handful when you were little, weren't you?"

Polly tsked. "What do you mean, when I was little? Still am. Are you with me or not?"

"Yes, but it'll take us at least an hour to get back to my truck and then over there."

"No problem. Come as soon as you can. I'll head there now."

By the time Harriet and Will arrived at the scene, the coast guard's helicopter was taking off. Harriet dashed over to Polly. "Did you talk to anyone about Clive?"

"Sure did. And they confirmed he worked with them. Sort of."

"What do you mean, 'sort of'?"

"They said they don't see much of him. They figured he must usually be on a different shift."

"Or like Rowena told Aunt Jinny, he travels a lot for work?"

Polly shook her head. "But they don't travel for work. I asked them. So he must be doing something else."

"Like spying, you mean?"

Will jolted at her question. "Spying?"

"You don't have to sound so shocked, Pastor," Polly said. "You said yourself that Clive seems to know more about a lot of things than most people."

Will raised an eyebrow at Harriet.

Heat rose to her cheeks. "I might have mentioned your observation about him to Polly. Was I not supposed to?"

"No, it's fine. That just wasn't what I meant with that observation." He paused, pressing his lips together, then said gently, "You can't go around blurting out suspicions like that. For one thing, if they happen to be true and the wrong person overhears you, they could put him or national security in jeopardy. And if it's not true, your suspicions could lead to a lot of unfounded mistrust and gossip."

Polly ducked her head. "We only told Van and Jinny the theory. No one else."

"How did Van respond?"

"Not well," Harriet said. "He said we shouldn't be concerning ourselves with Rowena's disappearance. But she kind of involved us when she abandoned her baby under our bush. And we seem to know more than Van does. He knew nothing about Detective Ascot, who questioned Rowena's neighbor."

"Although," Polly piped up, "if you ask me, Van knows more than he lets on."

Unable to sleep, Harriet wandered around the art gallery. Her grandfather had an incredible eye for detail and a gift for imbuing his scenes with an atmosphere or emotion that was almost palpable. She stared at the painting of a fishing boat heading out to sea in the early morning light and could almost smell the mist in the air, feel its dampness on her skin. His animal portraits revealed his deep connection to the creatures he cared for. Somehow, he managed through a twinkle in the eye or a trick of the light or a tilt of the head to depict the unique personality of every animal he painted, whether a dog or a horse or a goose or a goat.

She read the brief histories Mrs. Winslow had begun mounting beside some of the paintings, describing something special about the location or animal that inspired Grandad to paint the piece.

Some were details she'd gleaned from Grandad's journals, and others were from Mrs. Winslow's memory. Her heart warmed at the sight of Grandad's portrait that Mrs. Winslow had mounted in preparation for the weekend's reveal of *The First Unsteady Steps to Greatness.*

"Grandad, your life's work and your dedication to the welfare of the animals you treated are truly an inspiration," she whispered. "I hope I can live up to all you've entrusted to me."

She let herself into the storeroom, needing to assure herself that the painting was still there. She flipped on the wall switch, and light flooded the room. Holding her breath, she tugged the dustcover from the painting on the special easel Mrs. Winslow had found at an antique store specifically for the weekend's unveiling. The calf seemed to be gazing right at Harriet—a little fear eclipsed by the sense of determination beaming from his eyes.

She could relate. It was how she felt every time she heard whispers of why a local farmer called a different vet after years of trusting animals to her grandfather's care, or when an unhappy client refused to pay his bill.

As she stared at the painting, an eerie sense that she was missing something important crept into her mind. She recognized the old Henderson barn, standing off to one side in the background, more dilapidated now than the painting depicted. Dry stone walls delineated the curve of the hills.

She blinked, then squinted at the faint line running from one utility pole to the next across the field behind the barn. But there hadn't been any utility poles in the field when she'd walked there today. Her heart thudded. *It's the poles.*

She snatched her phone from her pocket and tapped Ned Staveley's name in her list of contacts.

A groggy voice answered the phone. "Hello?"

"Mrs. Staveley? I'm sorry to call so late." She glanced at the clock and cringed at the sight of the small hand pointing at midnight. "But I think I've figured out what made your cows sick. You once had utility poles in the field where your cows grazed. Is that right?"

"What?" she snapped. "You mean telegraph poles? Who is this?"

"Harriet Bailey. When were the telegraph poles taken down?"

"Some came down in a storm this past winter." The woman yawned noisily. "The electric company saw to having the line and poles removed just recently."

"I think they missed some. As you know, telegraph poles were treated with chemicals to keep them from rotting." A memory rose to Harriet's mind of the first day she drove to the Staveley farm. She'd passed workmen unloading the kind of equipment they might use to collect old telegraph poles. If that was what they were doing, it would explain the areas of flattened grass she and Will had seen.

"My husband's asleep. Can you call him in the morning?"

"Yes. I'm sorry again for waking you." Harriet hung up and smiled at the calf in the painting. "First steps," she whispered. Then she flicked off the light and returned to the house.

Too excited to sleep, she went to the study to search the internet for confirmation of her theory that the poles could carry lead. An hour and a half later she rubbed her dry eyes and sank back in her chair. She'd read article after article on the hazardous properties of the many chemicals used to treat wood against rot and insects, but she hadn't found a single mention of lead. While licking the wood may have made the cows sick, it didn't explain the elevated levels of lead in their blood. What was she missing?

Stifling a yawn, she reached for the mouse to shut down the computer. But as she did, a line in the description for one of the search engine hits caught her eye. It was for a health consultation for lead poisoning in cattle, in which an American farmer believed his cows had gotten sick due to recently sliced telephone poles.

Suddenly wide awake, Harriet clicked through and started reading. Her hopes rose with each page, wavering momentarily at the mention of also finding an old dump heap on the farm—a legacy of the previous owner. At the bottom of the page, their findings dashed her hopes. Testing showed no lead present in the telephone poles. So much for her brilliant deduction. British telegraph poles weren't likely to be treated with anything much different. Why had she called the Staveley house at midnight before checking her facts?

Snapping off the light, she called it a night and trudged off to bed.

Some detective she'd turned out to be. This week, they'd solved two mysteries—the case of the stolen painting that hadn't been stolen, and the case of the mysterious cow illness—without actually solving anything. She'd already suspected lead poisoning. The lab results merely confirmed it. But unless they found the source, the remainder of the Staveley and Vail herds could still succumb if she lifted their quarantine. That wasn't likely to win her any points with the local farmers.

And recovering the missing painting had simply made the question of what happened to Rowena more baffling than ever.

CHAPTER TWENTY-ONE

Harriet joined Polly in the clinic Friday morning more than a little bleary-eyed, without a single middle-of-the-night farm call to blame. "I thought I'd figured out what caused the lead poisoning in the Staveley cows and stupidly called him—at midnight no less—before doing my homework and figuring out that my brilliant theory wasn't so brilliant. Do you think it's too much to hope that Mrs. Staveley doesn't remember to tell her husband I called?"

Polly groaned in commiseration. "You know that finding the source isn't your job. He should be impressed you've spent so much time trying to track it down, given how stubbornly he refused to believe there could be anything dangerous in the field."

"I guess. It bothers me that we can't find the source, because it means we're almost certainly facing additional cases."

"And going above and beyond in that way would have been a nice boon for business."

The phone rang, and from the moment Polly snatched it up there was no mistaking Mr. Staveley's thick Yorkshire accent blasting over the line. Harriet reached for the receiver, but Polly backed away without relinquishing it. "Mr. Staveley, I believe she'll be able to fit you into her afternoon calls. But if it's urgent—" Polly held the phone away from her ear as Mr. Staveley bellowed that this afternoon was fine. "Right, she'll see you then." Hanging up the phone, Polly grinned. "He didn't say a word about telegraph poles. He has a pony that needs your attention. Apparently, you are now his go-to vet."

Harriet's spirits lifted. "That's something anyway."

The morning was quiet, giving Harriet time to help Mrs. Winslow prepare for Saturday's unveiling ceremony, which was back on.

"The mayor plans to come," Mrs. Winslow gushed. "He's always been a big fan of your grandfather's fishing boat scenes. Do you think we should ask him to cut a ribbon or something?"

"We could invite him to help with the unveiling. Perhaps ask if he'd like to say a few words."

"I'm so glad all the fuss over the theft was for nothing," Mrs. Winslow went on. "It was kind of that reporter not to print anything about it."

"Yes, I meant to ask you. Had you met Fraser Kemp before last week?"

"Not that I remember. Why?"

Harriet frowned, annoyed with herself for forgetting to ask sooner. But at the same time, she was skeptical that Kemp's interview request was any more pertinent to the mystery of Rowena's whereabouts than the recently removed telegraph poles were to the whereabouts of the lead source. "Kemp gave the impression he and Grandad went way back, but when an article on the gallery never materialized—at least not one that I've heard about—I couldn't help wondering if he said those things to win my trust."

"To what end, do you think?"

Harriet shrugged. "I'm a little afraid to imagine. It had crossed my mind that he might have been plotting his own art heist, only to discover that someone had apparently beaten him to it."

"And he had to assume we'd beef up security after that."

"Let's hope so." In reality, security updates were too expensive to consider at this point.

Polly called Harriet back to the clinic for a cat that had a run-in with a hay baler, leaving her no time to mull over either question. The cat appeared to be fine, but the owner wanted an expert opinion to be safe.

Harriet introduced herself to the slight young woman holding a furry bundle wrapped in a towel against her chest.

"I'm Maeve, and this is Marmalade," she whispered, her face as pale as her blond hair, which was dotted with strands of hay.

"It's nice to meet you. Why don't you tell me what happened while I examine Marmalade?" Harriet suggested as she lifted the bundle from the woman's arms.

"We recently moved here to help my father-in-law with his farm, and Marmalade isn't used to all the strange noises. But she loves mousing. We think that's what she was doing in the hayfield. Instead of running away from the baler, she crouched down out of sight. Fortunately, we stopped in time, but I'm worried about the effect it might have on her. You probably think I'm overreacting."

"Not at all." Harriet carefully pulled back the folds of the towel to reveal a very pregnant cat. "She may have been preparing to give birth in the field. You did the right thing by bringing her in, especially in her condition. I wish all owners were as attentive."

The poor creature quivered as violently as the last leaf of autumn clinging to its tree in the face of a stormy gale.

Harriet stroked her head and neck. "It's okay, Marmalade. We'll take good care of you." She used her stethoscope to listen to the cat's accelerated heart rate and breathing. After examining the extent of her injuries, which were surprisingly minimal, considering, Harriet suggested giving her a mild sedative that wouldn't harm the kittens to help relieve some of her anxiety. "After that, I suggest we keep her here for the day in a quiet, sheltered spot, so she'll feel safe to deliver. She's developing signs that her time could be imminent. This way we can monitor her if anything goes wrong."

Maeve looked relieved. "Whatever you think is best. I know my father-in-law will think I'm silly to go to all this expense over a cat when they're tuppence a dozen on the farm. But my husband and I haven't been able to have children, and Marmalade—" Her teary voice broke off.

"I understand."

"My husband is right torn up about it. He was driving the baler and blames himself for her being in danger, even though he's why she's okay." She pressed her palm to her lips and took a moment to collect herself. "I've never seen him so upset."

"You're most welcome to stay here with her if that will make you feel better. I'll ask Polly to make you a cup of tea, okay?"

"One step ahead of you," Polly declared, shouldering open the door with a tray of tea and biscuits in her hands.

Polly was a gem, and it hadn't taken her more than a week or two of them working together for her to know how best to render Harriet assistance in any given circumstance.

"Marmalade will be fine," Harriet said. She hoped she could say the same of the kittens. She hated to make promises she couldn't keep, which made her all the more apprehensive of the possibility she couldn't deliver on the promise she'd made to restore Benji's mother to him.

An hour later, she left the dozing cat under Maeve's and Polly's watchful care to attend to her afternoon farm calls.

Thankfully, the calls were all routine, and she worked through them quickly, leaving Goose Beck Farm for last. Before making the drive there, she called Polly to check on Marmalade.

"I was about to call you. Marmalade is the proud mother of four adorable little kittens, one named Bailey in your honor. I would have called sooner, but I knew you were busy, and I've handled this before."

Harriet laughed. "Wonderful. No trouble with the delivery?"

"None at all. Marmalade was a trouper and is already a great mother."

"Marvelous. I can't wait to meet them." Newly encouraged, Harriet sang along with the radio all the way to the Staveley farm, a route she now knew all too well. But hopefully, the farmer would soon have good news for her about the source of the lead that poisoned their cattle.

Mr. Staveley had taken in a pony for the summer for a couple traveling abroad. "She's gone lame in the hind foot," he said, leading Harriet to the large box stall where the Welsh pony was penned. Like the first time she visited the farm, the farmer's grandchildren soon lined the fence, watching her from between the wooden crossbeams. "I don't know much about horses myself. And I don't want to mess with one that isn't mine," Mr. Staveley went on, sounding a tad embarrassed by the admission. "The young ones have gotten quite attached to her, so I appreciate anything you can do."

"It's no trouble at all." Harriet soon found the culprit—a piece of wire stuck in the pony's hoof. She removed it and lifted her pliers to show the farmer and the children. "Here's our problem. I want to give her some antibiotics to ward off infection, but she should be as good as new in a few days."

The children clapped and cheered with glee, winning a smile from the gruff farmer.

As he walked Harriet out to her truck a few minutes later, he said, "The missus mentioned that you think the cows got sick from telegraph poles."

"I did think that, yes. The poles are coated with a cocktail of chemicals that could be hazardous to animals' health, but after further research, I couldn't find any documentation to confirm they actually contain lead. In fact, I found one study that found the exact opposite."

His shoulders slumped. "So it still isn't safe to send the cows back to pasture, even with the poles gone?"

"No, unfortunately. I'm sorry. I know it's not ideal."

"Vail found a pole that had rolled down to the beck that the men missed removing. He and his farmhand hauled it out of there this morning. I know you said there isn't usually lead in those, but what if that pole was an exception?"

"We could ask a field inspector to come and test it."

"I'd be right grateful."

"Okay, I'll look into it. Could you show me where the pole is?"

"Hop in." Staveley motioned to his four-wheeler, a small vehicle he obviously used to zip around the farm.

The kids, one step ahead of her, had already piled onto the rear. The eldest grandson opened a farmgate into the pasture then closed it again once they'd pulled through. The bumpy ride over the hilly rutted pasture was stomach churning, but the children shrieked in delight as their grandfather deliberately crested the hills with enough speed to cause their stomachs to drop.

His good humor vanished when he reached the back of what had been the Hendersons' old farmyard before Gilbert Vail acquired it. Mr. Staveley grumbled under his breath at the sight of the gate standing open between the common land and the farmyard. "Doesn't matter that we don't have cows out grazing." He drove into the farmyard then motioned to his eldest grandson to close the gate. "Vail knows better than to leave the gate open."

"The construction workers did it too," Abby piped up. "They left it open when they drove into the field to haul out the poles, and a lot of the cows wandered into the yard."

"You saw the cows in this yard?" Harriet asked her.

The girl ducked her head, sneaking a glance at her older brother, who shushed her beneath his breath.

"Answer the question, duck," her grandfather said gently. "We need to know."

She gulped. "You said we weren't to come to the barn. You said it was dangerous."

"That's right. I did. Because it is. But when you disobey, it's important to fess up."

"I told her she shouldn't be here," the older boy said.

"I saw the mama rabbit moving her babies into the barn, and I wanted to make sure they were all right, because you said it was dangerous and I didn't want them to get hurt."

"Did you see the cows in the yard?" Mr. Staveley pressed, clearly losing his patience.

"A bunch of them were wandering about. The men shooed them back after they dragged the poles out of the field."

"Did the cows seem to be interested in one area in particular?" Harriet asked hopefully.

The girl pointed, and Mr. Staveley drove in that direction.

"In an old farmyard like this, there could be any number of lead sources," Harriet told him. "It used to be in all kinds of things frequently used on farms."

"I know." Mr. Staveley set his jaw in a grim line, jumped from the vehicle, and strode around the corner of the dilapidated barn. "Henderson had an old dump heap over here." He kicked at a weed-infested pile of rubble then crouched and scrutinized the ground more closely. "I think we found our source." He picked up a stick and pointed to a pile of old batteries, paint, pipes, and other things Harriet would bet contained lead.

But her thoughts were stuck on the older boy's reaction to his sister and how he'd similarly shushed her last week when she'd asked after a missing cat.

Harriet's mind raced at the sudden recollection that the girl had said the cat had run under a bush at the vet's, where they'd found Benji. And was this where Abby had overheard the woman speaking on the phone? If the woman had lost her "cat" at Cobble Hill Farm, what was she doing here?

Harriet wandered around to the front of the barn. Noticing tire tracks through the weeds in the driveway, she asked the children, "Have you seen vehicles driving in and out of here?"

"Ramblers sometimes park in the drive to pick up the public path," Mr. Staveley said, his tone conveying his frustration with folks traipsing across the cow fields.

Ramblers like Mr. and Mrs. Rucksack, Harriet mused. "Is this where you overheard the lady mention losing her cat under the bush at the vet's?" she asked Abby.

The girl twisted her hands anxiously.

"Speak up, Abby," her grandfather ordered.

Abby admitted in a small voice that it was.

"Was she alone?" Harriet's heart raced, the gears spinning in her brain. Could it have been Rowena trying to get a coded message to her husband, letting him know where she'd hidden Benji before her kidnappers discovered she still had her phone?

Abby shook her head, avoiding eye contact.

"Two blokes came in with the woman between them," one of the boys supplied. "So we hid."

"Two men? Not an older man and woman?"

"No, two men."

Harriet's breath caught in her throat. "Can you remember anything they said?"

"They wanted her to ring her husband and tell him to give their friends something. But instead, she told him she lost their cat."

"Do you remember what they wanted him to give them?"

"We snuck out as soon as we could, before they said."

Mr. Staveley's face grew redder with every new detail the children divulged. "Why didn't you tell your grandmother and me about this?"

"Phillip told us not to because we'd get in trouble for being here," the girl piped up, nudging her oldest brother.

Mr. Staveley narrowed his gaze at the boy. "You know better than that. The woman could have needed help."

The squawk of a crow taking flight punctuated the remark. Could Rowena really have been so close? "When was the last time you saw a vehicle drive in here?" Harriet asked.

"This morning," Phillip said. "It was here when Mr. Vail went through with his tractor to fetch the pole. It took off as soon as he disappeared over the hill."

They'd been here *this morning*? Would Rowena's kidnappers have hung around the area so long, knowing everyone would be looking for her?

"I need to get to work," Mr. Staveley told her. "I'll let Vail know he needs to get this area cleaned up or fenced off and put a lock and chain on the pasture gate to make sure it stays closed."

"I'd like to poke around a bit more," Harriet said. "I can walk back to my truck."

"Suit yourself."

After the farmer sped off with the children, Harriet ducked into the barn to search for clues—anything that might give away where Rowena had been taken from here.

At the sound of voices filtering through the dusty shadows, she froze.

CHAPTER TWENTY-TWO

"Time's running out," a raspy male voice growled.

Harriet shrank into the shadows, straining to pinpoint where the man was.

"I already told you my husband works for the coast guard. He wouldn't have anything to do with smuggling antiquities."

Recognizing Rowena's voice, Harriet's breath stalled in her throat. If these men thought her husband was involved in an antiquity-smuggling ring, he must already be known to the criminal world as someone who could be bought. Or he was a criminal himself.

"And I'm telling you he'd better call off the watchdogs who do then," the raspy voice replied.

Watchdogs? If Clive was a smuggler, why would he have the ear of anyone who was in charge of guarding valuable antiques? Harriet pulled out her phone and texted Van. I'm at old Henderson barn. Rowena being held here. I think only one kidnapper present, and without transport. Then she silenced her phone so notification of his response wouldn't give away her position.

When no response came within a minute or so, she texted again. Are you coming?

Still no response.

"You have the wrong man," Rowena insisted, sounding a lot calmer than Harriet imagined she'd be if their positions were reversed. "My husband is not part of the Secret Intelligence Service."

"Are you sure? Maybe he's kept you in the dark too. Spies do that."

The Secret Intelligence Service, more commonly called MI6, was the British equivalent of the CIA. Perhaps their theory that Clive was a spy wasn't so far off. They clearly weren't the only ones who suspected as much.

"Or maybe," the man said in a venomous tone, "his mission is more important than his wife. And when Jenkins gets back with the kid, we'll know if it's also more important than his son."

"No!" Panic ripped through Rowena's voice.

Harriet looked frantically at her phone. Why wasn't Van responding? She sent a text to Polly, explaining what was happening and where. She asked her to call 999, the emergency number in the UK, and to warn Aunt Jinny that someone might be coming for Benji.

Polly's reply came within seconds. CALLING THEM NOW. WE WILL KEEP BENJI SAFE. DON'T DO ANYTHING FOOLISH.

Harriet pocketed her phone and squeezed under a fallen roof timber to try to spot Rowena's exact location. Her captor must have a gun on her or surely she would have shouted for help when they heard the four-wheeler drive up. Hopefully, now that it had driven off once more, the captor would let his guard down, assuming they'd escaped detection.

"What guarantee does my husband have that you will release me if he turns a blind eye to the smuggling?" Rowena asked.

The man cackled. "So you're finally admitting it's within his power now, are you? You can be proud of yourself that you held out for a full week."

"If my husband *is* what you say"—Rowena's voice quavered with emotion—"I clearly have no influence over his actions, or he would have done what you wanted by now."

"Fortunately for you, transport was delayed, but if he doesn't let the shipment through tonight—well, I'm sure I don't have to go into detail, do I?" The man's tone left no doubt about the intended consequences of not cooperating.

A wind whipped through the barn, stirring up ancient dust.

Smothering her mouth, Harriet fought the urge to cough. But just when she thought she'd conquered the impulse, she let loose a deafening sneeze. Fearing the worst, she grabbed the closest thing at hand to use to defend herself—an ancient milking stool missing a leg.

There was sudden silence, confirming her fear that they'd heard her.

Then a blood-chilling creak like a rusty hinge broke the silence. A trapdoor rose from the dirty floor. A skinny, dark-haired man wearing a dingy T-shirt and grimy jeans emerged from the cellar beneath the barn.

Keeping one eye on the man, Harriet edged as quietly as she could toward the door she'd come in. She jumped when she backed into a stored pitchfork, sending it clattering to the ground.

"Who's there?" the man growled.

Harriet tossed the broken stool and snatched up the pitchfork. "The police are already on their way," she declared, forcing a bravado into her voice she didn't feel.

The sound of an approaching engine diverted his attention for an instant, and she dashed for the door. She saw Gilbert Vail coming across the dales in his four-wheeler, no doubt having been told by his neighbor about the hazardous mess he needed to deal with.

Harriet raced toward him, waving the pitchfork over her head to get his attention. "Help! Over here!"

"Stop!" Harriet's pursuer ordered from behind her. "Don't make me shoot you."

Harriet stopped running and slowly turned around.

"Good. Now throw that pitchfork over here." He'd moved along the outside of the barn wall to get closer to her, keeping out of Gilbert's line of sight. After she complied, he said, "Now, here's what's going to happen if you don't want your farmer friend shot."

The sound of approaching police sirens echoed over the dales.

"You're too late." Harriet held up her hands in surrender, silently praying he didn't decide to go out with guns blazing.

Gilbert roared up in his four-wheeler and parked. Harriet knew the exact moment he caught sight of the gun. His eyes widened, and he demanded, "What's this about?"

"Get over there. Both of you." The guy flicked his gun barrel, directing them away from the vehicle.

Gilbert held up his hands but seemed frozen to the spot.

"Now!" The gunman shot at his feet, kicking up dirt.

They hurried in the direction he'd pointed, and he jumped on Gilbert's four-wheeler. "Keys," he snapped.

Gilbert tossed him the keys, but they fell far short of the man's position. The flash in the farmer's eyes made her think that was deliberate.

The approaching sirens grew louder, joined by the thump and slap of chopper blades slicing the air.

The man lunged for the keys, and Gilbert hauled Harriet behind the cover of the barn.

But by then the gunman didn't seem to care about anything but escaping. He kicked the vehicle into gear and took off over the dales.

"He was holding a woman in the cellar." Harriet dashed into the barn, where she found Rowena with her hands and feet bound, struggling to reach the ladder out of the cellar. Harriet and Gilbert hurried down to help her.

Gilbert sliced the ropes with a pocketknife. "Let's get you out of here."

Rowena gripped Harriet's arm. "Benji. My baby. Is he okay?"

Harriet pulled her into a hug. "Safe and sound. He'll be so happy to have his mommy back."

Tears flooded the woman's eyes, and her legs buckled.

Harriet and Gilbert managed to keep her upright and assisted her up the ladder.

Rowena rubbed at the marks on her wrists. "How did you find me?"

Harriet grinned. "You can thank some wayward cows, whose mischievousness made them sick, and an animal-loving little girl who was worried about your lost cat."

"My lost cat? Oh dear, I haven't given our poor cat a single thought."

"Your neighbor is taking care of that. One of Mr. Staveley's granddaughters said she overheard you tell your husband your cat ran under the bush outside my clinic."

Understanding lit Rowena's eyes. "I was trying to tell him where Benji was. I wasn't sure until today if my kidnappers knew about him." Rowena squinted against the bright light as she emerged into the sunshine.

Three police cars swerved into the driveway, followed by Polly's car, while the helicopter hovered low over the field.

Gilbert shielded his eyes. "I think the chopper is going after the bloke who stole my quad."

Van rushed up to them, along with several armed officers. "Is everyone okay?" he asked.

"He got away on my quad." Mr. Vail pointed to the field.

"He won't get far." Van turned to Rowena. "How are you, Mrs. Talbot?"

"Rattled. But I'll be much better once I see my baby."

Aunt Jinny sprang from the back seat of Polly's car and dashed toward them, toting her black medical bag, while Polly and Will followed more sedately, with Benji nestled in the pastor's arms. Harriet grinned at the sight.

"Benji," Rowena cried. She sprinted past Aunt Jinny straight to Will, who transferred the infant into his mother's arms. "Oh, sweetie, I missed you so much." She smothered his head and face with kisses then held him close, pressing her cheek to his downy head. Benji cooed and giggled.

"That reunion is better medicine than anything I could've given her," Aunt Jinny said.

Suddenly remembering why this wasn't over, Harriet told Van, "There was a second kidnapper—Jenkins. He was trying to get to Benji."

Van nodded. "We got him. The keen-eyed lad who helps in your barn recognized and intercepted him for us."

"Good for Alfie."

A report came over Van's shoulder-mounted radio. He acknowledged it then said to Harriet and Gilbert, "The helicopter pilot's fancy flying trapped Rowena's kidnapper against a stone wall, and the officers aboard subdued him without incident."

The helicopter that had disappeared from sight behind a distant hill rose into the air once more.

Mr. Staveley also appeared in the field on his four-wheeler, no doubt curious what all the excitement was about. A moment later the helicopter touched down on a bare patch beside the barn, and a young man jumped from the side door.

"Clive?" Rowena gaped as the man raced toward mother and child.

He swept both of them into his arms. "I'm so sorry. So very sorry."

"You didn't give them what they wanted, did you?" she asked.

He brushed the hair from her cheek and gently whisked away a tear with his thumb. "It didn't come to that, but I would've given them anything they asked for if I thought it would keep you safe."

She leaned her cheek into his palm. "I know you would have."

Polly sidled over to Harriet. "I guess he's not a criminal, huh?"

Harriet chuckled. "Nope. But I suspect you might've nailed him with your second theory."

Polly's face lit up. "Really?"

Harriet shrugged. "Not that it matters. Something tells me even if they admit to being security agents of some sort, we're not going to be allowed to talk about it."

"Still, it'll be fun to know, even if we have to keep it to ourselves."

Uniformed police were already cordoning off the area, and several plainclothes officers swarmed into the barn.

Polly pointed to two men climbing from another vehicle. "Those are the two guys from the Crow's Nest. They're with the police?"

"Looks like it," Harriet said, a little taken aback by how unthreatening they seemed now that she knew they weren't the enemy.

Paramedics persuaded Rowena to sit in the rear of the ambulance so they could assess her condition with Aunt Jinny's supervision. Clive stood nearby with Benji, clearly unwilling to allow his wife or son out of his sight for even a moment. Sergeant Adam Oduba, a handsome young officer from Ghana, took Gilbert's statement, and Van took Harriet's.

Van soon wrapped up his questioning and urged her, along with Polly, Aunt Jinny, and Will, to go home.

"That's it? We don't get to find out what this was all about?"

Van gave her a dry smile. "It's above my pay grade to decide that. But I can tell you for sure that you won't find out right now."

As they headed to Polly's car, a black SUV with tinted windows drove in, and Clive steered his wife toward it.

"Oh, they'll need the car seat." Aunt Jinny unfastened it from the back of Polly's car.

"I'll take it to them." Harriet scooped the seat from Aunt Jinny's grip and strode over to the SUV.

The driver stepped out and opened the rear door for her.

Recognizing him, even in the dark sunglasses, she stumbled.

Clive caught her arm. "Careful. Here, let me take that." Without waiting for her response, he relieved her of the seat and buckled it into the back of the vehicle.

Harriet returned her attention to the driver. "Not so fast, Fraser Kemp. Is that even your real name?"

With his index finger, he tugged his sunglasses down to the tip of his nose and winked. "Sorry I never got an article about the unveiling of your grandfather's painting into the local paper for you. By all accounts, you and he both deserve that."

"So you *are* a reporter?" she asked, injecting a heavy dose of skepticism into the question.

He shrugged. "When I need to be." He pushed his sunglasses back up his nose, got into the driver's seat, and pulled his door closed.

"Who was that?" Will asked as she returned to Polly's car.

"I'm not really sure." Holding on to the passenger door with one foot already in the car, she glanced over the car's roof at the beehive of activity around the Hendersons' old barn. She could picture where the calf had stood when Grandad captured his image, not far from where Rowena's kidnapper had trained his gun on her. In that moment her legs had felt as wobbly as a newborn calf's.

But she'd kept her promise to Benji, and that was more important than laying everyone's secrets bare.

CHAPTER TWENTY-THREE

Saturday dawned sunny and bright. A light breeze off the sea filled the air with its fresh, briny scent.

Charlie pounced on Harriet's bed at the crack of dawn and then played obstacle course when she got up, twining around her legs wherever she went. When she showered, the cat sat outside the bathroom door and yowled. Then when Harriet finally sat down to eat her breakfast, Charlie jumped up onto her lap and kneaded her thighs.

She scratched the back of the cat's neck. "I know you miss Benji, but he needs to be with his parents."

She heard Aunt Jinny call her from the front door, where she must have let herself in.

"I'm in the kitchen," Harriet called back.

Aunt Jinny appeared in a flowing white sundress with bright blue flowers and a fancy hat worthy of the horse races.

"Wow, what are you all dressed up for?"

"The grand unveiling, of course. Aren't you going to put on your best togs?"

Harriet chuckled. "I suppose I should. To be honest, my mind was so preoccupied last night with the exchange I overhead between Rowena and her captor that I dressed by rote this morning." Harriet lifted Charlie down from her lap. "And this one hasn't helped. She's been out of sorts since Benji left."

Aunt Jinny stroked Charlie's fur. "I can relate. It was lovely to have a baby around again. They grow up too fast."

Maxwell scampered in, his back wheels clunking into the chair leg.

Harriet gave him a dog biscuit. "I think Maxwell is happier though." She scratched behind the dachshund's ears. "You were feeling left out with our flitting over to Aunt Jinny's all the time, weren't you?"

Aunt Jinny removed her hat and helped herself to a cup of tea. "Well, things should get back to normal around here now. And I daresay that with the stellar impression you made on Gilbert Vail and Ned Staveley—by ferreting out the source of the lead that made their cows sick and a criminal hideout to boot—more of Dad's old clients will be clamoring to meet the incredible new Doc Bailey."

Harriet's cheeks heated. "All I ask is that they give me a chance."

"You don't have to worry about that." Polly swept into the room, also dressed to the nines. "My brother said Gilbert was at the pub last night singing your praises. I bet your exploits will reach legendary proportions before the weekend's out."

"Gracious," Harriet said, heat creeping into her cheeks. "What are they saying about why Rowena was kidnapped? If Clive really is with secret intelligence, as her kidnappers seemed to think, it'll blow whatever cover he hoped to have around here. They may have to move."

Aunt Jinny paused with her teacup halfway to her lips. "I'm sure any agency he's with is quite capable of spinning a story to suit the narrative they need people to believe."

"It's kind of scary when you think about it." Polly plunked into a seat on the opposite side of the table and helped herself to a slice of toast. "That they can so easily dupe the public."

"I would hope they merely bend the truth enough to keep their operatives and their families safe," Harriet said. "I can sure see why Rowena might have felt blue after Benji's birth, knowing the danger Clive's job could bring to their doorstep."

Polly glanced at the time. "Shouldn't you be getting dressed? The unveiling is in an hour, and the field Alfie marked off for parking is already filling up. He and the oldest two Danby kids are doing a smart job of directing traffic."

"Doreen recruited a dozen ladies to bake scones for the event as a fundraiser for the RNLI," Aunt Jinny added. "I hope you don't mind that I said it would be okay."

"That's a fabulous idea," Harriet assured her. "You two go on ahead. I'll catch up."

As Polly and Aunt Jinny headed out, chattering merrily, Harriet watched them with a smile. It was nice to look forward to a pleasant event for a change.

Preferring to avoid the limelight, Harriet invited the mayor to conduct the unveiling. To Harriet's surprise, her grandfather had saved the mayor's little dog from being trampled by a spooked horse when he was a child, prompting the mayor to pay him a touching and heartfelt tribute before pulling the cover from the newest addition to the gallery. He urged Harriet to say a few words, but Harriet managed to defer the privilege to Ida Winslow by inviting her to share the story behind *The First Unsteady Steps to Greatness*.

As Harriet stepped away from the podium, Aunt Jinny whispered, "You won't escape that easily."

Mrs. Winslow gave a colorful telling of Grandad's experience helping to birth the calf in his painting. "He'd often recount how he'd feared he didn't have the strength or endurance to pull the little fellow out in time. You see, his head was turned back, as was one foot, with only one small hoof pointing the way it should."

She gave a dramatic pause, taking the opportunity to bask in the rapt expressions of her audience.

"He used to say it's a chronic problem humans have too. We start heading the way we should go, even make a positive step or two in that direction. But the instant things get difficult, we begin to doubt our decision. We look back instead of keeping our eye on the goal. We might even consider making an about-face. We think it might be better to stay where we know what to expect rather than venture into a whole new world of experiences we can't even imagine."

Harriet could think of at least one recent example of that in her own life.

"But with the urging of his mum and the guidance of the caring man in front of him, the brave little fellow finally found his way out. Although he needed a bit of help getting to his feet, with the help of a few good friends, he soon took those first steps toward greatness." She motioned to the painting with a flourish. "Because, as many of you know, the bull depicted in this painting is our beloved Roscoe, who went on to sire some of the finest cattle in our county."

The crowd broke into applause. Some older men called out the names of the cows they credited to Roscoe.

Harriet leaned close to Aunt Jinny's ear. "I had no idea Mrs. Winslow was such a gifted orator."

"Many of us have had the privilege of getting to know a lass who has similarly shown a tremendous amount of courage and perseverance as she finds her footing in a strange, and at times hostile, new land." Mrs. Winslow directed a stern glare at two or three men in the crowd.

Tracking her friend's gaze, Harriet spotted a farmer who had made it clear that he wasn't thrilled she'd taken over her grandfather's practice. He was the last person she'd expected to see here. Never mind that farmers in general weren't known for taking Saturdays off, except maybe for a tractor show.

"Thankfully for us," Mrs. Winslow continued, "she's not easily dissuaded. And as Old Doc Bailey did for Roscoe, many good folks have come alongside to offer her guidance and encouragement. Because where would we be without our newest Doc Bailey at the helm of Cobble Hill Veterinary Clinic?"

Taken aback at the praise, Harriet blinked. "She was talking about me?"

"Of course, silly." Polly pushed Harriet forward as the crowd burst into thunderous applause.

"Speech, speech," Will shouted, echoed by many others throughout the room.

Dumbfounded, Harriet bit her bottom lip as she stared at the boisterous group. "I'm afraid I'm not nearly as gifted a speaker as our dear Mrs. Winslow. But I hope I can make up for that whenever you have a pet or farm animal in need of my care. My grandfather bequeathed me a tremendous legacy, and as Mrs. Winslow so aptly described, I have often felt like that wobbly young calf as I've struggled to familiarize myself with all the new and wonderful things that make Yorkshire God's Own County."

That earned her a few whistles and whoops.

"*He* is truly the one who brought me here. And who brought so many lovely people into my life who, when I've been tempted to turn back, urge me to have courage and step forward."

Once again, the crowd burst into applause. Harriet waved and thanked them.

Neighbors and tourists alike pressed forward to shake her hand and thank her for all she'd done. Harriet wasn't sure what exactly they were referring to—her veterinary work or yesterday's apprehension of the kidnappers, the news of which had probably done as much to draw visitors to today's event as the painting. And she thought it wise not to ask.

One of the highlights was when Allen's father pulled her aside and apologized for his sharp reception earlier in the week, and even commended her foresight in quarantining Mr. Staveley's cattle.

"Wow," Aunt Jinny said after he left. "You've clearly made an impression."

After the crowd thinned, Clive and Rowena approached Harriet in a quiet corner of the gallery. Benji was fast asleep against Clive's chest, his small body dwarfed by his father's large hands.

"We wanted to thank you for everything you did," Clive said. "DC Worthington told us that you helped Dr. Garrett care for Benji and relentlessly followed up on every clue that presented itself in an effort to find my wife."

Harriet pressed her lips together, uncertain how to respond. "I'm glad you're both all right," she said finally.

"Yes." Rowena rested her hand on Clive's arm. "And Clive's hunting for a new job. One that keeps him home more."

Harriet tilted her head, unable to contain the smile that played on her lips. "Is it true? What those criminals thought you did for a living, I mean."

"If it was, I wouldn't be at liberty to say, now would I?" Clive asked.

To be fair, Harriet hadn't expected an actual verbal confirmation. "There's just one thing I can't figure out. Fraser Kemp, the guy who drove you home yesterday? He made the appointment to interview me about my grandfather's painting before we'd even reported Rowena's disappearance to the police. How'd he know?"

"The kidnappers contacted me within an hour of taking Rowena. I feigned a bad connection and kept saying I couldn't hear them, which caused them to say a lot more than they probably intended."

"How did you know to hide Benji?" Harriet asked Rowena.

"When your aunt wasn't here for Benji's appointment, I walked him around the grounds. I happened to pass by the barn, where I overheard the two men scheming inside. I pretended I needed the loo when I brought Benji to your clinic so you'd know who he was if I had to hide him on your property. It set my mind at ease that he took to you so quickly. But I couldn't leave him with you then, because what if they looked in the windows and saw a baby with Clive's hair?"

"I can't exactly deny him," Clive agreed, ruffling his own mop of red hair.

"So I hid him in the bushes and prayed someone would find him if I, well, couldn't return to him right away," Rowena said, swallowing hard. "Then I sneaked back to the barn to see if I could glean any other information to pass on to Clive, but they caught me that time. They let me make a phone call about our 'cat,' but that was all."

"I don't know how you held yourself together," Harriet said to Rowena. "You must have been so scared."

"Yes and no. I don't know how to explain it, but I managed to keep my focus on God instead of the men, and He gave me an inexplicable peace. I trusted that He would keep my son safe and that everything else would go according to His divine plan. And it did. I can't give too many details, but the authorities have been able to do a lot with what I learned while I was in captivity."

"No matter how dark things seem, there's always hope." Clive wrapped an arm around his wife and kissed the top of her head.

Polly joined them and said, "So after the bad guys had Rowena call you, you told your people to send guys like Fraser Kemp to scout around for clues and put up the motion-detector cameras?" She turned to Harriet. "Which, by the way, were removed this morning."

"My people?" Clive's eyes twinkled. "I called the authorities, yes. And Dr. Garrett's voice mail assured me Benji was safe."

"Right." Harriet nodded. "I just have one piece of advice for you," she said to Clive.

He shifted Benji in his arms. "What's that?" he asked.

"Next time you burn something, make sure you burn *all* of it."

Clive looked a little startled. Then he laughed. "I'll keep that in mind." He winked and led his family away.

"You think he meant it when he said he's job hunting?" Harriet asked Polly.

Polly snorted. "He really said that? I wasn't under the impression that sp—I mean, guys like him changed professions all that often. They might station him closer to home to support his cover, but I very much doubt he's actually changing jobs."

"On the other hand, it's obvious he cares about his family. His bosses probably know he would have caved to keep Rowena safe, which would make him a security risk, right? They probably suggested the change."

"If you say so," Polly replied in an arch tone. "Though I suppose we'll never know for sure."

"And that's the truth," Harriet said. "Let's get back to the party. Mrs. Winslow put so much work into it that it would be a shame to miss anything."

As they mingled with the crowd, Harriet reflected on Aunt Jinny's words from earlier that morning. Yes, things would certainly get back to normal, but around Cobble Hill Farm, that never meant boring.

FROM THE AUTHOR

Dear Reader,

Researching and writing this story has been an incredible journey of discovery for me. Although my parents were both born and raised in the UK, I'd never visited it. So when Guideposts invited me to write a story for the Cobble Hill Farm series, I seized the opportunity to explore my roots and experience Harriet's new life in Yorkshire for myself.

I grew up watching the original *All Creatures Great and Small* TV series based on James Herriot's veterinary adventures, but being there was beyond what I could have imagined. Walking through the dales among the ewes and their lambs, the cows and their calves, exploring centuries-old barns and even older ruins, navigating narrow roads flanked by classic drystone walls, and admiring vistas colored with bright yellow gorse bushes—all to the sounds of pheasant calls, ringing church bells, and bleating sheep—opened my eyes to an abundance of story possibilities.

I was blessed to be chauffeured about by my intrepid brother-in-law, UK native Grahame Chandler, whom I can't thank enough for organizing our accommodations and sparing me from having to learn how to drive on the opposite side of the road. But trust me, I experienced enough of the narrow, steep roads from the passenger side to feel Harriet's struggle to navigate the moors, and in a manual vehicle, no less.

Over and above that, Grahame arranged for me to interview a real vet from the modern TV series *The Yorkshire Vet*. I'm so grateful for how generously Shona shared her time and expertise with me. Across the countryside of Yorkshire—from shopkeepers to farmers, to folks whose gardens we inadvertently crossed after wandering from the public path—all were incredibly friendly and helpful in answering my questions and passionate about sharing their stories.

I discovered the idyllic countryside my mother came to love when evacuated from London as a child during World War II. And I heard stories from my uncle Allen of their later life on a farm—the chicken with the broken leg (that I gave Allen in the story) being my favorite.

I learned about such things as the smuggling routes of a bygone era in the seaside town of Robin Hood's Bay and the selfless men and women who volunteer with the Royal National Lifeboat Institution to save lives at sea. I learned about miners and fisherman and even farmers, who had to reinvent themselves in the face of mine and woolen mill closures, collapsing fisheries, and devastating cattle diseases—men and women who, like my grandparents before them following WWII, found the strength and courage to carve a new way of life for themselves. And I witnessed the fierce pride of the Yorkshire people, pride in their land and in their heritage.

Each person's story helped inspire Harriet's own journey in this story and her growing confidence that if she puts her trust in the Lord, no matter how dark things look, there is always hope.

Signed,

Sandra Orchard

ABOUT THE AUTHOR

Sandra Orchard writes fast-paced, keep-you-guessing stories with a generous dash of sweet romance. Touted by Midwest Book Reviews as "a true master of the [mystery] genre," Sandra is also a best-selling romantic suspense author. Her novels have garnered numerous Canadian Christian writing awards, as well as an RT Reviewers' Choice Award, a National Readers' Choice Award, a Holt Medallion, and a Daphne du Maurier Award of Excellence. When not plotting crimes, Sandra enjoys hiking with her hubby, working in their vegetable gardens, and playing make-believe with an ever-growing brood of grandchildren. Sandra hails from Niagara, Canada, and loves to hear from readers.

TRUTH BEHIND THE FICTION

O n the first day of August in Yorkshire towns and villages across
the UK's largest county, streets, homes and businesses are
adorned with bunting and Yorkshire flags for their annual Yorkshire
Day celebrations. This is the day when the people of Yorkshire celebrate the rich culture and heritage of the county that spans nearly
three million acres, proudly dubbed God's Own County or even
God's Own Country.

An important part of the celebration is the declaration of the
Yorkshire Day Pledge, which proclaims that "Yorkshire is three
Ridings (jurisdictions) and the city of York, with these Boundaries
of 1,145 years standing; That the address of all places in these ridings is Yorkshire; That all persons born therein or resident therein
and loyal to the Ridings are Yorkshiremen and women" and so on.

Each year a different city or town is designated as the host town
for the celebration. Traditionally, the region's mayors and other
public figures gathered there for a breakfast reception before meeting for a thanksgiving service. These days, however, events take
place across the region in the form of street parties, concerts, fairs,
parades, and fundraising activities for charity,

The date of August 1 was chosen for the special day because two
important events in Yorkshire's history took place on that date. One

was the Battle of Minden in 1759, in which the King's Own Yorkshire Light Infantry played a prominent role, along with other British and German forces, in driving the French army from what is now Germany. The Yorkshire soldiers wore the traditional white rose on their caps that adorns Yorkshire's flag (a white rose on a blue background). Also on August 1, in 1833, the Slavery Abolition Act, championed by Yorkshire MP William Wilberforce, was passed.

Over the decades since its inception, Yorkshire Day has become an opportunity for people from all over Yorkshire to come together and celebrate the distinctive culture and history of the county.

YORKSHIRE YUMMIES

Bilberry Pie

Ingredients:

For the pastry:

scant 2 cups pastry flour   8–9 teaspoons cold water
½ cup butter

For the filling:

3½ cups bilberries* (In North America,
   substitute blueberries or huckleberries)
¾ cup white sugar

Directions:

1. Preheat oven to 375 degrees.
2. Cut butter into flour until crumbly then sprinkle with water to form into a ball. Let rest in cool place for 30 minutes.
3. Divide pastry in half then roll out half to line 9-inch pie plate.
4. Fill with berries and mix in sugar.
5. Roll out pastry top and cover pie. Dampen and seal edges, trimming excess.

---

*Bilberries are also called moorland berries, wimberries, or European blueberries. They are a close cousin to North American blueberries, but smaller and more acidic.

6. Prick center of top with a fork to allow steam to escape.
7. Bake until pastry is golden-brown and crisp.

Hint: Best served hot with custard or cold with whipped cream.
Popular Variation: Bake bilberries in a Yorkshire pudding batter.

Read on for a sneak peek of another exciting book
in the Mysteries of Cobble Hill Farm series!

Three Dog Knight

BY JOHNNIE ALEXANDER

The brown-and-white Mini Lop rabbit, though wrapped in a fleecy doll blanket, shivered as Harriet Bailey passed him to young Winifred on this Tuesday afternoon in September.

The ten-year-old girl cuddled her new pet in her arms, holding him close as she stroked one of his silky-soft ears. The gesture reminded Harriet of another young girl who often popped into her prior veterinary clinic with a rabbit or a hedgehog or an orphaned possum—whatever the child found in her countryside wanderings. Harriet never knew what to expect when the shoebox lid was dramatically lifted to reveal the injured creature inside.

Both girls had blond hair, intense blue eyes, and sharp features. They might have been sisters, except they lived an ocean apart—one in rural Connecticut and this one on a farm a few miles outside the charming Yorkshire village of White Church Bay, England.

"It's an awful thing people do to these bunnies." Alma Wilkerson placed a comforting arm around her daughter's thin shoulders. "Buying them as pets then abandoning them when their tykes grow tired of caring for them. The poor things don't know how to live in the wild."

"At least this one has found a home." Harriet gave Winifred a reassuring smile while her insides burned with frustration. She'd recently found a year-old newspaper article in Grandad's archives about an area in West Yorkshire where rabbit rescue groups were overwhelmed with the problem. Apparently, the media attention had done nothing to curb the inhumane practice.

Harriet met Alma's gaze and prayed her well-intended words wouldn't cause offense. "A pet should never be an impulse," she said. "Though perhaps this one is an exception to the rule."

"That it is, and you needn't worry," Alma assured her. "We already have quite the menagerie at our place, and a more motley collection you've probably never seen. One more will make little difference. Why, it was my own boy, Walker, who brought Maxwell to Old Doc Bailey. We'd have kept him too, except Doc fell in love with the pup."

At the sound of his name, Maxwell's ears perked up. The black-and-tan long-haired dachshund had followed Harriet into the examination room and greeted the Wilkersons with happy barks. His back legs had been paralyzed when he was hit by a car, but Harriet's grandfather had outfitted him with a wheeled prosthesis, so the dog had little trouble getting wherever he wanted to go.

Now he was the official clinic dog—a fun surprise included in Harriet's inheritance of Cobble Hill Farm, which encompassed her grandfather's nineteenth-century house, art gallery, and veterinary practice. She'd also been given stewardship of Charlie, the official office cat. After she'd been rescued from a burning trash bin as a kitten, Grandad had adopted her too, making her the latest in a long line of clinic cats named Charlie. Harold Bailey had always insisted that giving them all the same name gave him one less thing to remember.

Charlie's sweet temperament made her a delight to have around. Despite her physical scars, or perhaps because of them, Harriet thought the muted calico was one of the most affectionate cats she'd ever come across.

"Grandad enjoyed Maxwell's company," Harriet said. "And I do too." Especially on those occasional evenings when Connecticut felt as distant as the moon and she second-guessed the wisdom of her radical move to Yorkshire.

"I'm naming him Toffee, and he'll stay in my room," Winifred asserted confidently. She focused her intense blue gaze on Harriet. "He'll be okay now, won't he?"

"You did everything you could for him," Harriet replied. "Keeping him warm, feeding him, and cleaning that nasty wound. And I've done everything I can."

"Giving him medicine," Winifred said.

"That's right." Harriet had treated the wound on Toffee's haunch and suggested vaccinations as well as an antibiotic. "So now it's up to Toffee to get better."

Winifred's features softened as a huge smile lit her face. Reassured that the Mini Lop had found his forever home, Harriet ushered the little girl and her mom from the examining room to the empty reception area. Maxwell dutifully followed behind them.

"I hope we didn't keep you from any plans," Alma said as she paid the bill. The Wilkersons had arrived with the injured rabbit a minute before the clinic closed. Polly Thatcher, the receptionist, usually locked up, but she'd already left due to an eye appointment.

"Nothing that couldn't wait," Harriet replied. "I'm closing early today because Aunt Jinny and I are taking items to the Antique Festival for the appraisal exhibit."

Harriet's paternal aunt, a local physician, lived in the dower cottage that had once been part of the farm. Her husband, Dominick, had died of a heart attack about ten years before, and her son lived with his wife and two children in nearby Pickering. The entire family had welcomed Harriet with open arms when she arrived.

"We're going to the festival too, aren't we, Mum?" Winifred practically bounced with excitement. "I'm going to ride the Ferris wheel and eat cotton candy and all kinds of stuff."

"That's for later," Alma said. "After the chores are done."

"And after I get Toffee settled," Winifred agreed more seriously.

"I was surprised when Aunt Jinny told me about the carnival," Harriet said. "When I first heard about the festival, I thought it was specifically an antique show."

"It started out that way." Alma tucked her debit card into her wallet. "Quite like the program on the telly where people bring in old items to see if they have any value. As the years went by, the committee added the rides, food vendors, and entertainment. It's all different than it used to be except for the name. That hasn't changed, but that's because of Ivy and Fern, the infamous Chapman sisters."

"I've met Fern but not Ivy." Harriet printed Alma's receipt and stapled it to her invoice.

"Those two are oil and water. Always have been." Alma raised her eyes to the ceiling as if seeking divine assistance, and Harriet, who'd had her own entertaining interactions with Fern Chapman, hid a smile.

"Ivy has been on the Antique Festival committee since its beginning, and she came up with the name," Alma continued. "As the event became more successful, Fern insisted on being involved too. She couldn't let Ivy get all that praise year after year, could she?"

Harriet chuckled. "Some sisterly truths are universal."

"That they are. Anyway, each year Fern makes a motion at the planning meeting to change the name, and each year that motion goes down in flames. The other members vote against Fern to keep Ivy happy. They have to keep Fern happy too though, so when she makes a motion to add something new to the event, they agree. This year it's a dunk tank."

"That sounds entertaining." Though she wanted to be diplomatic, Harriet still found it difficult to reconcile Ferris wheels and dunk tanks with the upscale appraisal event she'd envisioned when she read the festival's promotional materials. Those hadn't mentioned carnival rides and fair food. Not that she was opposed to either.

"It's fun for the children," Alma agreed. "Even though Ivy's initial dream of a premier antique show with a national reputation gets dimmer while the event grows beyond the name, she's too stubborn to change it to something more fitting."

Harriet couldn't pretend to know the inner dynamics of the Chapman sisters' relationship, but her sympathies were with Ivy. The carnival rides and games were surely fun for the community, but Ivy must be disappointed to see her dream of an event that celebrated history and legacy overshadowed by something altogether different.

When Aunt Jinny invited Harriet to attend the festival with her, she'd mentioned that local residents often learned surprising historical details about the treasures stowed away in their attics. The previous year, Miss Jane Birtwhistle, retired schoolteacher and feline aficionado, had brought in a vase to be appraised and almost had a heart attack when the appraiser valued it at over five thousand pounds. Most items weren't worth nearly as much, except in sentimental value. Still, it was all good fun, and Aunt Jinny had encouraged Harriet to find something to take to the event.

Once the Wilkersons were on their way with cheery goodbyes, Harriet locked the clinic door and flipped the sign from Open to Closed. While she tidied up, she glanced at a decades-old photograph of Grandad, when his hair was still dark and he sported a moustache, standing beside a famed racehorse whose care had been entrusted to Old Doc Bailey and no one else.

Hundreds of similar photos were in albums of various sizes in Grandad's study—Old Doc Bailey with prize bulls and sheep, bottle-fed calves and foals, dogs, cats, guinea pigs, a variety of reptiles and birds, and even chickens—lovingly compiled by Grandma Helen, who had died of cancer before Harriet was born. Aunt Jinny had maintained the tradition of taking and preserving photographs of her father.

Perhaps, Harriet should have taken a selfie of herself with Winifred and her new bunny. In the age of digital photographs, it might be nice to create photo albums of her own to add to the Bailey legacy.

She hung her white lab coat on its designated hook then opened the door connecting the clinic to the kitchen so Maxwell could enter in front of her. Though she'd moved to the farm a few months before, she still found it difficult to believe the stone Georgian-style house and all its contents belonged to her.

Of course, that meant all the inconveniences that came with outdated plumbing, heating, and electrical systems belonged to her as well. Strange how those issues that had seemed so overwhelming when she first arrived were now mere annoyances.

Though she loved everything about the decor of her new house, Harriet had added a few personal touches of her own, including a framed montage of five photographs that adorned an open space on the kitchen wall. She paused to soak in the memories ignited by those photos. Her favorite showed her parents standing beneath a giant sycamore tree on a beautiful sunshiny day. They'd been oblivious to the click of Harriet's digital camera as they shared the kind of smile that came with decades of happy marriage.

How she missed seeing them every day. The ache for home tugged at her heart, its suddenness bringing tears to her eyes. How could she have left Mom and Dad, everything she'd known and loved, to move thousands of miles away? At the time, when she was in such despair, the news of the inheritance had seemed an answer to prayer. An excuse to escape.

But ever since she'd received the invitation from the Whitby Women's Society to speak at their monthly luncheon in less than two weeks, she'd been bombarded with thoughts of what she'd left behind when she'd said goodbye. Her heart was heavy with a longing not only for a home but for *home*.

Going back, however, was impossible. How could she after Grandad had entrusted his beloved home, his veterinary practice with its odd assortment of eccentric clients, and his paintings to her keeping? She believed herself to be more of the steward of his legacy than the new owner of all that was once his, and she intended to honor and protect what he'd devoted his life to build and then passed along to her.

An ornate wall clock chimed the quarter hour, and Harriet jumped. She'd been so lost in her thoughts that the minutes had ticked by without her. She hurried to the entryway, where a golden umbrella stand, a porcelain peacock figurine, and a blue-and-white delft pitcher were displayed on a side table. Harriet had chosen each item as a possible contender, but she couldn't decide which of the three to have appraised at the festival.

A knock sounded on the door as it opened. "It's me," Aunt Jinny called. She smiled at Harriet as she entered the house. She wore a pale yellow sweater—which she would call a jumper—and pleated trousers. A blue-and-green paisley scarf completed the outfit.

"I'm sorry I'm running late," Harriet said. "I had a last-minute rabbit emergency."

"The Wilkersons? I saw their car pulling out and guessed you'd been held up. But I'm the last person you need to apologize to when it comes to medical emergencies." Though she was nearing retirement age, Aunt Jinny's family practice kept her busy. "I've lost count of the number of times I've missed the opening hymn at church."

"Winifred found a Mini Lop this morning by their mailbox," Harriet explained. "Poor little guy had a gash on his leg and was scared half to death."

"Are the Wilkersons keeping him?"

"Thankfully, yes, and Winifred has named him Toffee. She's taking his care very seriously. Otherwise, I suppose the clinic would have had a new mascot. He's cute, but a clinic dog and an office cat are enough for me to keep up with to say nothing of any boarders or overnight patients."

"Speaking of, where are Charlie and Maxwell?"

"I imagine Charlie is curled up in a patch of sunshine somewhere. And Maxwell headed to Grandad's study after the clinic closed. He likes lounging in there sometimes." Harriet waved at the side table. "Will you help me decide what to take to the festival? I thought the pitcher because it seems most likely to be worth something, but maybe not. I have no idea where it came from."

As an artist himself, Grandad had a keen eye and impeccable taste. But he also had a playful, whimsical side and was known to browse what the British called jumble sales for anything that caught his eye, even if the item had no intrinsic value. That made it difficult for Harriet to know which collectibles scattered around the immense house were valuable and which ones had simply struck Grandad's fancy. Neither did she know which items he'd collected and which ones he'd inherited from his own parents. Or even his grandparents.

The Bailey family had been at Cobble Hill Farm since the house was built in 1820. A portrait of Harriet's great-great-grandfather hung on the landing of the stairs that led to the second floor. His name was Harold too, but, unlike Grandad, the first Harold appeared stony and cold in his portrait. None of Grandad's photographs showed him with an icy demeanor, and no one would ever describe Old Doc Bailey in any way but warm and good-humored.

Perhaps Harriet should take Harold's portrait to the festival for an expert opinion on its value. But unless the artist, a name Harriet didn't recognize, was famous, the frame was probably more valuable than the painting.

Aunt Jinny considered for a moment then said, "Take the umbrella stand. Dad hates it, but it was a gift from a friend."

Harriet smiled at how Aunt Jinny sometimes talked about her father in the present tense, as if he were still with them.

Looking around the entryway and into the adjoining reading nook, she couldn't help feeling that perhaps he was part of the crowd of witnesses mentioned by the writer of Hebrews. After all, this house was still much more Grandad's than hers with its dark woods and leather furnishings.

"The umbrella stand it is then," Harriet said. "I'll get a box."

A short time later, the golden stand with its floral design was safely stored next to a hideous gargoyle about the size of a shoebox in the trunk of Aunt Jinny's sporty red Renault Clio. The gargoyle had the eroded appearance of a chiseled stone that had been exposed to a century of inclement weather.

"Where did that come from?" Harriet asked.

Aunt Jinny's eyes sparkled as she closed the trunk which she'd call the boot. "He was tucked away in a corner of the attic, but don't ask me how he got there or where he came from, because I don't have the answer to either of those questions. I went to the attic to see what treasures I could find, and he was there. And now he's here." She waved her hand in a dramatic gesture over the Renault's trunk. "I've named him Winston."

"Winston? After Churchill?"

"Who else? I think the former prime minister would be honored and amused."

"Do you think it's worth anything?" Harriet tried to keep the doubt from her voice but failed miserably.

Aunt Jinny's good-natured laugh was the warm hug Harriet needed to shoo away the unsettled ache surrounding her. She laughed too, though she couldn't say why, as she slid into the front passenger seat and fastened her seat belt, while congratulating herself for not accidentally sliding into the driver's seat. By the time she was able to visit her parents, she'd probably think their cars were the weird ones.

Aunt Jinny drove to the spacious public meadow that overlooked the pounding waves of the North Sea where community events were commonly held. Colorful banners and decorated tents dotted the grounds. Food booths vied for attention with carnival games. Calliope music from a few of the rides were periodically drowned out by the shouts of excited children. Other rides, such as the Ferris wheel, were in the final construction stages.

A large pavilion in the center of the meadow hosted the festival's main event—at least, its *intended* main event. Aunt Jinny explained that the interior had been transformed into a museum where all the antiques were displayed on shelves or in glass cabinets. The experts appraised the items on their own then selected certain ones to showcase. Though they scheduled time to talk to each owner about his or her contribution, only their conversations with the owners of the showcased antiques were filmed by a local video production company.

Harriet and Aunt Jinny carried their items to the pavilion, stopping several times along the way to greet friends and neighbors.

Sometimes it seemed to Harriet that her aunt knew everyone in Yorkshire and had been present at the birth of many of them. Eventually, they reached the registration area, where Ivy Chapman reigned behind a waist-high counter on the veranda outside the pavilion's huge double doors.

"There you are, Dr. Garrett," Ivy said to Aunt Jinny. "I can't wait to see the worthy antique you brought for the appraisers. And this must be your niece, the American veterinarian I've heard so much about. My sister, Fern, said you worked miracles with that nasty old goat of hers. Why Fern keeps that aged animal is beyond me. I suspect it's mostly to spite me. She's so perverse. As soon as I advise her one way, she goes the other. I've never known the like from anyone else. Show me what you have, and I'll get you registered."

Harriet's eyes had widened with each new sentence that Ivy uttered without taking a breath. Even if Alma Wilkerson hadn't mentioned that Ivy and Fern were sisters, Harriet would have guessed they were closely related. Both women appeared to be in their mid-fifties and had auburn hair, striking green eyes, and slender figures.

Fern had said nothing about a sister when Harriet visited her small farm to tend to the pet goat a few weeks ago. In fact, Harriet was certain that Fern, who was as talkative as Ivy, had given the impression she was an only child whose parents had died several years before. She'd had a beau when she was young, but they'd quarreled, and she vowed never to give her heart away again. Fern had advised Harriet to make the same promise to herself.

Even though Harriet had recently experienced her own broken heart, she wasn't about to make that vow. Though, strange to say, she wasn't as sad about the end of her engagement as she'd been a few months ago. The death of her grandfather had overshadowed that loss, and the details of a permanent move from the United States to England had taken much of her attention. To her surprise, her heart was mending sooner than she'd thought possible.

The registration process didn't take long with Ivy in charge. She had much to say about Aunt Jinny's gargoyle—none of it flattering—and she gushed over the uniqueness of Harriet's umbrella stand. They were given receipts for their items and a packet with information about the appraisal process and schedule.

"She called poor Winston ugly," Aunt Jinny said when they were out of earshot. She feigned offense then laughed as she led the way to the food booths. "It's a gargoyle. He's supposed to be ugly."

"I'm relieved she liked my umbrella stand." After hearing Ivy's critique of the gargoyle, Harriet had been hesitant to remove her item from its box. "She's going to be more disappointed than I will if it turns out to be from some big-box store."

"Not all of those are bad. I like several of them, actually." Aunt Jinny directed Harriet to the Biscuit Bistro booth and introduced her to Poppy Schofield, the fortyish woman behind the table. Harriet no longer needed to remind herself that a British biscuit was an American cookie.

She was trying to decide between a Cornish fairing, which was a spiced ginger biscuit perfect for autumn, or an Empire biscuit, a Scottish iced cookie with raspberry jam, when her aunt's conversation caught her attention.

"It's a mystery to be sure," Poppy was saying to Aunt Jinny. "And not only my store has been bothered. Mr. Calabash walked into his insurance agency one morning to find that all the pictures in his office had been moved around. Not a one where he usually had them."

"That sounds like a prank to me," Aunt Jinny replied. "Are you sure that incident is related to the theft at your store?"

"Only those responsible know," Poppy said. "I've talked to DC Worthington, and he agrees it's mighty mysterious for someone to break in and do such a thing. I wouldn't have minded so much if they'd taken the orange floral cookie jar, as it was never one of my favorites, but for a thief to take the coral rose one—that's simply unforgivable. I intended to bring it for the appraisal exhibit, and now I can't. The perpetrator must be found."

Harriet's heart pounded. Since she'd moved to the charming village of White Church Bay, she'd been embroiled in one mysterious adventure after another. She prayed Aunt Jinny was right, that Poppy's theft and Mr. Calabash's prank were typical small-town mischief.

But something in the air—and it wasn't the bracing wind from the sea—sent a shiver up her spine. So-called harmless pranks often weren't viewed that way by the victims. And if the same pranksters were also thieves, what might they decide to do next? Who would be their next target?

A NOTE FROM THE EDITORS

We hope you enjoyed another exciting volume in the Mysteries of Cobble Hill Farm series, published by Guideposts. For over seventy-five years, Guideposts, a nonprofit organization, has been driven by a vision of a world filled with hope. We aspire to be the voice of a trusted friend, a friend who makes you feel more hopeful and connected.

By making a purchase from Guideposts, you join our community in touching millions of lives, inspiring them to believe that all things are possible through faith, hope, and prayer. Your continued support allows us to provide uplifting resources to those in need. Whether through our communities, websites, apps, or publications, we inspire our audiences, bring them together, and comfort, uplift, entertain, and guide them. Visit us at guideposts.org to learn more.

We would love to hear from you. Write us at Guideposts, P.O. Box 5815, Harlan, Iowa 51593 or call us at (800) 932-2145. Did you love *Into Thin Air*? Leave a review for this product on guideposts.org/shop. Your feedback helps others in our community find relevant products.

Find inspiration, find faith, find Guideposts.
Shop our best sellers and favorites at
guideposts.org/shop

Or scan the QR code to go directly to our Shop

**Loved Mysteries of Cobble Hill Farm? Check out
some other Guideposts mystery series!**

SECRETS FROM GRANDMA'S ATTIC

Life is recorded not only in decades or years, but in events and memories that form the fabric of our being. Follow Tracy Doyle, Amy Allen, and Robin Davisson, the granddaughters of the recently deceased centenarian, Pearl Allen, as they explore the treasures found in the attic of Grandma Pearl's Victorian home, nestled near the banks of the Mississippi in Canton, Missouri. Not only do Pearl's descendants uncover a long-buried mystery at every attic exploration, they also discover their grandmother's legacy of deep, abiding faith, which has shaped and guided their family through the years. These uncovered Secrets from Grandma's Attic reveal stories of faith, redemption, and second chances that capture your heart long after you turn the last page.

History Lost and Found
The Art of Deception
Testament to a Patriot
Buttoned Up
Pearl of Great Price
Hidden Riches

SAVANNAH SECRETS

Welcome to Savannah, Georgia, a picture-perfect Southern city known for its manicured parks, moss-covered oaks, and antebellum architecture. Walk down one of the cobblestone streets, and you'll come upon Magnolia Investigations. It is here where two friends have joined forces to unravel some of Savannah's deepest secrets. Tag along as clues are exposed, red herrings discarded, and thrilling surprises revealed. Find inspiration in the special bond between Meredith Bellefontaine and Julia Foley. Cheer the friends on as they listen to their hearts and rely on their faith to solve each new case that comes their way.

The Hidden Gate
A Fallen Petal
Double Trouble
Whispering Bells
Where Time Stood Still
The Weight of Years
Willful Transgressions
Season's Meetings
Southern Fried Secrets
The Greatest of These
Patterns of Deception

The Waving Girl
Beneath a Dragon Moon
Garden Variety Crimes
Meant for Good
A Bone to Pick
Honeybees & Legacies
True Grits
Sapphire Secret
Jingle Bell Heist
Buried Secrets
A Puzzle of Pearls
Facing the Facts
Resurrecting Trouble
Forever and a Day

MYSTERIES OF MARTHA'S VINEYARD

Priscilla Latham Grant has inherited a lighthouse! So with not much more than a strong will and a sore heart, the recent widow says goodbye to her lifelong Kansas home and heads to the quaint and historic island of Martha's Vineyard, Massachusetts. There, she comes face-to-face with adventures, which include her trusty canine friend, Jake, three delightful cousins she didn't know she had, and Gerald O'Bannon, a handsome Coast Guard captain—plus head-scratching mysteries that crop up with surprising regularity.

A Light in the Darkness
Like a Fish Out of Water
Adrift
Maiden of the Mist
Making Waves
Don't Rock the Boat
A Port in the Storm
Thicker Than Water
Swept Away
Bridge Over Troubled Waters
Smoke on the Water
Shifting Sands
Shark Bait

Seascape in Shadows
Storm Tide
Water Flows Uphill
Catch of the Day
Beyond the Sea
Wider Than an Ocean
Sheeps Passing in the Night
Sail Away Home
Waves of Doubt
Lifeline
Flotsam & Jetsam
Just Over the Horizon

Find more inspiring stories in these best-loved Guideposts fiction series!

Mysteries of Lancaster County

Follow the Classen sisters as they unravel clues and uncover hidden secrets in Mysteries of Lancaster County. As you get to know these women and their friends, you'll see how God brings each of them together for a fresh start in life.

Secrets of Wayfarers Inn

Retired schoolteachers find themselves owners of an old warehouse-turned-inn that is filled with hidden passages, buried secrets, and stunning surprises that will set them on a course to puzzling mysteries from the Underground Railroad.

Tearoom Mysteries Series

Mix one stately Victorian home, a charming lakeside town in Maine, and two adventurous cousins with a passion for tea and hospitality. Add a large scoop of intriguing mystery, and sprinkle generously with faith, family, and friends, and you have the recipe for *Tearoom Mysteries*.

Ordinary Women of the Bible

Richly imagined stories—based on facts from the Bible—have all the plot twists and suspense of a great mystery, while bringing you fascinating insights on what it was like to be a woman living in the ancient world.

To learn more about these books, visit Guideposts.org/Shop